Gc
929.2
B681905b
1941247

REYNOLDS HISTORICAL
GENEALOGY COLLECTION

ACKNOWLEDGMENTS

In preparing these historical records for publication, I want to mention some of those who so greatfully furnished me with records which I would not have been able to include if it had not been for their assistance.

Cousin John J. Bowman of Liberty, Missouri has furnished me with a mass of information which his father the Reverend, Thomas Anderson Bowman had compiled and written some forty or fifty years ago, when he attempted to compile and publish a family history, but did not finish. His Biographys have been written mostly in the present tense.

Another cousin Joe Bowman of Sikeston, Missouri has also been a great, great help in furnishing additional information concerning our fore-fathers.

Dr. Paul H. Bowman of Timberville, Virginia, now a retired President of Bridgewater (Virginia) College, having served in that capacity from the year 1919 to 1946, and he is in the same generation as the writer of this history, he too has furnished the writer with information concerning his branch of the family.

Then too there are all of the individuals who have been so kind, and generous in furnishing additional information concerning dates and addresses. Those who co-operated so beautiful in answering the many letters I have written to ascertain such information sought.

To THESE, and those which I have personally mentioned, I can not find words adequate enough to express the magnitude of gratitude I owe to each of you.

And especially to each of you who have written me so many personal letters expressing your explicit gratitude for my efforts expended in bringing the history to a final completition.

Sincerely,

Byron W. Bowman.

1941247

INDEX

Information concerning the following INDEX

The following Index will give the names, their last address, their occupation of all those whom we have received the proper information.

The Index shows the year born, and died, if dead. The pages upon which a descendant will be found giving the record of their birth, or death, to whom married, and that of their children living or dead.

It will also give their ancestral record number, so far as our records go.

When a number occured in (parenthesis) it means that it is either the wife, or the husbands' number of a certain direct BOWMAN ancestor.

There may have occured errors in our compilations, but if so, remember we have tried diligently to eleminate all errors posible. And would appreciate your prompt advise concerning same so that our records can be changed, so that we may issue corrections to those who may have reserved a copy of the history.

Dec! means deceased.
Bio! means Biography.

Residential addresses will no doubt change from time to time, and a letter addressed to a member of this large family may be returned by the postal authorities. If this should happen just drop me a post card, and I will see if I can give you a more recent address.

I have tried to make this history informative, and have recorded in its entirety every descendants back from the third to the eighth generations, and a good portion of those of our immediate fore fathers back as far as the first and second generation, which we were enabled to obtain.

I am sure that some of the biographies of the early ancestor will be very much enjoyed by all.

Sincerely,

August 22, 1956.   *Byron W. Bowman*
                      Historian.

YEAR BORN-DIED	A	Pages	Record No.
1912-	Abbott, Wilda Virginia Smythe 2801 Olympic Drive, Bakersfield, California.	55,75,147,148,	446
1909-	Abbott, Cloyd Gale 2801 Olympic Drive, Bakersfield, California. (Dehydrator Operator, Ring Oil Co.)	55,75,148	(446)
1946-	Abbott, James Darwin, 2801 Olympic Drive, Bakersfield, California.	75,148,	566
1927-	Axtell, Barbara Louise Bowman 420 West Beauegard Ave, San Angelo, Texas.	59,78,180,	464
1922-	Axtell, Jay M. 420 West Beauegard Ave, San Angelo, Texas.	59,78,181,	(464)
1944-..,	Axtell, Ronnie 420 West Beauegard Ave, San Angelo, Texas.	59,78,181,	585
1947-	Axtell, Tony 420 West Beauegard Ave, San Angelo, Texas.	78,181,	586
1870-1938	Abernathy, Thomas Alexander Sr	21,38,192, Dec!	(227)
1942-	Abernathy, Charlsie Lou 718 Columbia St, Springfield, Ill.	63,202	486
1880-1955	Abernathy, Anna Bowman	21,38,102-A Dec!	227
1918-	Abernathy, Edythe Whitehead 718 Columbia St, Springfield, Mo.	39,62,202	(363)
1946-	Abernathy, Peggy Ann 718 Columbia St, Springfield, Ill.	63,202,	487
1916-	Abernathy, Thomas Alexander Jr 718 Columbia, Ill. (Salesman Clothing)	39,62,193,202,	363
1882-1912	Alexander, Bessie Beulah Bowman	23	248

B

1834-1895	Baldridge, Robert	20,31,101,104, Dec!	216
1879-1947	Baldridge, Herbert	31,50,104,105, Dec!	320
1881-1943	Baldridge, Irene (Portis)	31,50,104,108, Dec!	321
1889-	Baldridge, Robert Lee 4948 Page Blvd, St Louis, Mo.	31,50,104,111,	322
1885-	Baldridge, Alice Elizabeth Lalumendier, 4948 Page Blvd, St Louis, Mo.	31,50,111,	(322)
1882-	Baldridge, Mary Ellen Storm Windsor, Illinois.	31,50,105,	(320)
1909-	Baldridge, William Herbert Greenup, Illinois.	50,68,105,106,Bio 106-A	416
1913-1943	Baldridge, John Harold	50,105,107 Dec!	417
1917-	Baldridge, Margaret H. Carrell Greenup, Illinois.	50,68, 106	(417)
1951-	Baldridge, Robert Sam Greenup, Ill	68,106	522
1914-	Baldridge, Estella Mills	50,107	(417)
1920-	Baldridge, William Joseph M/Sgt 37625396.A.B.Group Hq Sg Sec 18th,APO 239 San Francisco, California In Okinawi.	50,69,111,113,	421

Born-Died	B (Continued)	Pages	Record No.
1922-	Baldridge, Geraldine V. Stoff	50,69, ,113,	(421)
1942-	Baldridge, William J, 2nd	69,113,	527
1948-	Baldridge, Sandra Ann	69,113,	528
1954-	Baldridge, Dennis J	69,113,	529
1892- ?	Bellamy, Franklyn Howlett	55,150,	(336)
1901-	Banes, Louella Abernathy (McNabb) 6318 Evergreen Ave, Berkley 21, Missouri.	38,61,194,195,	358
1893-1952	Banes, Charles Henry Dec'	61,	(358)
1916-	Bennett, Mary Irene Welker P.O. Box, 190, Arnold, Missouri.	40,64,	370
?	Bennett, Edward	40,64,	(370)
1804-1873	Bowman, Benjamin, Dec'	Bio' 10, 11,12,	33
1804-1896	Bowman, Sophia Ferguson, Dec'	Bio' 13,14,	(33)
1827-1897	Bowman, Lucy Ann (Chapman) Dec'	Bio' 18-A,12,	103
1829-1859	Bowman, Elizabeth Mary (Henley) Dec'	Bio' 19-B,12,	104
1831-1837	Bowman, Charles Chisholm, Dec'	12,	105
1833-1838	Bowman, John Otea, Dec'	12,	106
1835-1837	Bowman, William Edwin Dec'	12,	107
1837-1920	Bowman, Benjamin LeRoy (Lee) Dec' (Final resting place Sikeston, Mo Mausoleum.)	Bio'102-A,12,20,	108
1840- 1930	Bowman, Eliza Jane Ford Dec' (Final Resting place Sikeston, Mo Mausoleum.)	Bio' 108,12,20,	(108)
1839-	Bowman, James Orin Dec'	12,	109
1841-	Bowman, Carroll Dec'	12,	110
1843-	Bowman, Samuel Sterling Dec' (Taft, Florida last record of Residence)	Bio'21-A, 12,	111
1846-1888	Bowman, Sophia Perizade (Welker)(Pope) (Marquand, Mo last record of Residence)	Bio' 21-B,12,	112
1850-1915	Bowman, Thomas Anderson Dec' (Last resting place Jackson, Missouri)	Bio' 21-C,21-D,21-E,12,23,	113
1850-1918	Bowman, Sarah Emma, Gholson Dec'	Bio'21-F,12,23	(113)
1857-1899	Bowman, Amy Sophia (Baldridge)Dec'	20,31,101,104,	216
1859-1950	Bowman, William Chesley Dec' (Last resting place Sikeston, Mo Mausoleum.)	Bio'115-A,115-B,20,31,114,101	217
1861-1906	Bowman, Charles Christopher Dec' (Last resting place Dexter, Missouri)	Bio' 139,20,33,101,138,	218
1863-Inf	Bowman, Mary Lee Dec'	20,101,	219
1866-1948	Bowman, Nettie (Jordan) Dec' (Last resting place Little Rock, Arkansas)	20,34,102,156,	220
1868-1949	Bowman, Samuel Lee Dec' (Last Resting place Dermott, Arkansas)	20,35,102,159,	221
1871-1927	Bowman, Annie Gherman	35,159,	(221)
1880-1956	Bowman, Edna McCloy, (Leeper) Dec (Last resting place Dermott, Arkansas)	35,20,162-A,	(221)
1870-	Bowman, James Reed 318 Florence St, Jackson, Mo. Ret. Treas Cape County Milling Co.	Bio'163-B,21,35,102,163,	222
1872-1935	Bowman, Thomas Ford Dec'	21,36,103,174,	223
1875-1878	Bowman, Lou Ella, Dec'	21,102,	224
1877-1952	Bowman, Joseph Maple Dec' (Resting place Brady, Texas)	21,36,102,177,178,	225
1878-1940	Bowman, Wilbur Talley Dec'	21,37,103,186,	226
1880-1955	Bowman, Anna (Abernathy) Dec'	21,38,103,192,	227
1884-Inf	Bowman, Franklin Dec'	21,103,	228
1873-	Bowman, Lillie B.(Lively) 318 Florence St, Jackson, Mo.	20,35, 163,	(222)

Born-Died	B.	Pages	Record No.
1864-1938	Bowman, Emma Estes, Dec' (Last resting place in Sikeston, Mo, Mausoleum.)	20,31,114,	(217)
1853-1935	Bowman, Martha Emeline Whitener (Bedford) Dec (Last resting place Dexter, Missouri)	20,33,	(138)
1883-	Bowman, Lillie Donaldson Dec'	21,36,177,	(225)
1882-1955	Bowman, Minnie I. Brodnax Dec'	21,36,178,	(225)
81-	Bowman, Hattie Donaldson 1051 Post St, Apt 26, San Francisco, California.	21,37, 186,	(226)
2-1953	Bowman, Minnie Marie Van Doren Dec' (Last address 1414-A E DeSoto Ave, St Louis 7, Mo)	21,36,174,	(223)
	Bowman, Lyman Russell Sr (Res. Sikeston, Mo. Pres. Scott County Mlg Co, Chairman Board)	31,51,114,116,	323
1954	Bowman, Hita Claudia Gilbreath Dec'	31,51,114,116,	(323)
	Bowman, Joseph (Sikeston, Mo; Sup't Scott County Mlg Co)	32,51,114,121,	325
	Bowman, Margaret E. Vaughn (Sikeston, Mo)	32,51,121,	(325)
18	Bowman, Lee Reed (Sikeston, Mo; V-Pres, General Sales Manager Scott County Milling Co.)	32,52,114,124,	326
1897	Bowman, Verna Ester Cox (Sikeston, Missouri)	32,52,114,124,	(326)
1893-	Bowman, Samuel Schuyler, Sr (Sikeston, Mo; Rep. Allied Adjustment Bureau)	32,52,115,127,	327
1894-	owman, Illa Fowler (Sikeston, Missouri)	32,52, 127,	(327)
1896	Bowman, Arnold Paul Dec' (Last resting place Sikeston Mausoleum)	32,53,115,131,	328
1895-	wman, Margaret Emily Dover	32,53,131,	(328)
1899-	wman, Robert Byron (Sikeston, Mo; Dir. & Purchasing Agent, Scott Co Mlg Co)	32,53,115,134,	329
1899-	wman, Ruby Evans (Sikeston, Missouri)	53,134, 134-A	(329)
1907-	man, William Chesley Jr Sikeston, Mo, Sales Mgr Flour Div, Scott Co Mlg Co)	33,54,115,137,	332
1907-	an, Ellen Sanderson Sikeston, Missouri)	33,54,137,	(332)
1934-	B an, William Chesley, 3rd ouston, Texas, C/O Shell Chemical Co.)	54,137,	440
1935-	Bo an, John Sanderson (keston, Mo; Student, Junior, Alabama U, Tuscaloosa,)	54,137,	441
1907-	Bow n, Lyman Russell Jr (keston, Mo; Chemist Scott Co Milling Co)	51,69,116,117,	422
1907-	Bowm n, Lida Bell Powell (Skeston, Missouri)	51,69,116,117,	(422)
1931-	Bowma , Jack Powell (Skeston, Mo: or U.S.A.F. Box A-36-40th FIS APO:328 an Francisco, Calif He is in Japan)	69,117,	530
1934-	Bowma , David Gray (Sikeston, Mo; Present a student in Alabama U, Tuscaloosa, Alabama.)	69-117,	531
1920-	Bowman, Benjamin Lee (Sikeston, Mo; Manager Grain Dep't Scott Co Mlg Co)	51,70,116,119,	424
1920-	Bowman, Rita Laurie Heisserer (Sikeston, Mo)	51,70,116,119.	(424)
1948-	Bowman, Steven Paul (Sikeston, Mo)	70,119,	533

-B- (Continued)

Year	Name	Numbers	Record
1952-	Bowman, Laurie Lee (Sikeston, Mo)	70,119,	534
1919-	Bowman, Lt Col, John Webster (U.S. Marine Corp, Honolulu, Hawaii. Stationed after July 1, 1956)	52,71,124,125,	420
1924-	Bowman, Eleanor Noyes Hempstone (See Record No above #420 for address)	52,71,125,	(420)
1944-	Bowman, John Webster, Jr (See #541 for address)	71,124,125,	541
1947-	Bowman, Ellen Hempstone (See # 541 for address)	71,125,	542
1950-	Bowman, William Cox (See # 541 for address)	71,125,	543
1923-	Bowman, Lee Austin (Sikeston, Mo; Sales Mgr Feed Division, Scott Co Milling Co.)	52,71,124,126,	429
1927-	Bowman, Cathleen Carpenter (Sikeston, Mo)	52,71,124,126,	(429)
1949-	Bowman, Camille (Sikeston, Missouri)	71,126,	5
1952-	Bowman, Lee Austin Jr (Sikeston, Missouri)	71,126,	
1953-	Bowman, Marilyn Cox (Sikeston, Missouri)	71,126,	
1915-	Bowman, Sam Schuyler, Jr (1745 E. Horne St, Salt Lake 6, Utah. Land Dep't of The Texas Company,)	52,72,127,128,	
1915-	Bowman, Josephine Evelyn Hopper (1745 E. Horne St, Salt Lake City 6, Utah.)	52,72,128,	(430)
1915-1935	Bowman, Julia Mattie Fenimore Dec'	52,72,128,	430)
1935-	Bowman, Samuel Schuyler, 3rd (Sikeston, Mo; At present a Senior Engineer sent, Rolla (Mo) School of Mines, Rolla, Mo.)	72,128,	547
1948-	Bowman, David Paul (1745 E. Horne St, Salt Lake City 6, Utah.)	72,128,	548
19 51-	Bowman, Philip Lee (1745 E. Horne St, Salt Lake City 6, Utah.)	72,128,	549
1917-	Bowman, Sgt. Eugene Fowler (Present address Sikeston, Mo; now in Air Force at Anderson Field, Guam.)	52,72,127,129,129	431
1917-	Bowman, Rosemary Tallent	52,72,129,	(431)
1924-	Bowman, Dorothy Mae Henthorn (Address with husband in Guam.)	52,72,129-A,	(431)
1945-	Bowman, Dorothy Ann (With parents in Guam)	72,129-A.	552
1948-	Bowman, Peggy Lee (With parents in Guam)	73,129-A,	553
1937-	Bowman, Carol Jean (Student at Texas A & M College, Bryan, Texas.)	72,129,	550
1942-	Bowman, William Morrell (With parents in Guam)	72,129,	551
1920-	Bowman, Arnold Paul, Jr (121 N. Prospect Ave, Madison, Wisc. Chemist & Ass't to Production Mgr, Oscar Mayer Meat Co.)	73,131,133,	434
1920-	Bowman, Jean Linville Welke (121 N. Prospect Ave, Madison, Wisconsin.)	53,73,133,	(434)

-B-

5.	Mary Linville 73,133,	556	
1944-	(21 N.Prospect Ave,Madison,Wisc.)		
	., Melissa Hamilton 73,133,	557	
1948-	(121 N.Prospect Ave,Madison,Wisc.)		
	an, Phillip Dover Dec' 53,131,	435	
1926-194	...dan, Nancy Ann 53,134,	437	
1938-	(Present address Sikeston,Mo, Entering Lindenwood College Sept 1956. St Charles, Mo.)		
	...owman, Curtis Burette Dec' 33,54,138,140, 333		
188/	(Present Resting place Eudora,Ark, was Secty & Gen. Mgr, Dermott Gro & Comm Co.)		
	Bowman, Dee Dysart 33,54,140, (333)		
	(Address Eudora, Arkansas)		
1891	Bowman, Claud Whitener, Dec' 33,54,138, 334		
	(Resting place Marquand,Mo.)		
140-	Bowman, Byron Whitener 145,33,54,138,142, 335		
	(Eudora,Ark.Pres.B.W.Bowman Co,Inc) Flour - Feed and Grain Business.		
93-1920	Bowman, Ruth Bernice Blankenship Dec' 54,142, (335)		
	(Resting place at Dexter, Missouri)		
116-	Bowman, Charles Dale 55,74,142,143, 443		
	(1545 Martin Ave,C.P.Birmingham 8, Alabama; Car Distributor, Birmingham Southern R.R.		
118-	Bowman, Sally Mable Pass 55,74,143, (443)		
	(1545 Martin Ave,C.P. Birmingham 8, Alabama.)		
1940-	Bowman, Charles Whitener 74,143, 560		
	(1545 Martin Ave,C.P.Birmingham,8 Ala.)		
1943-	Bowman, James Patrick 74, 143. 561		
	(1545 Martin Ave,C.P. Birmingham 8,Ala.)		
1899-1952	Bowman, Lillie Mae Shehorn,Dec' 54,145, (335)		
	(Resting place Dexter,Missouri.)		
1923-	Bowman, Byron Burette 55,74,146, 445		
	(1020 South Frederick St, Arlington,Virginia; (Transportation Intelligence Department of Army.)		
1927-	Bowman, Lethea Ann Davis 55,74,146, (445)		
	(1020 So. Frederick St, Arlington,Virginia.)		
1949-	Bowman, Teresa Ann 75,146, 564		
	(1020 So.Frederick St, Arlington,Va.)		
1954-1956	Bowman, Melinda Sue,Dec' 75,146, 565		
	(1020 So.Frederick St, Arlington,Va.)		
1912-	Bowman, Samuel Lee, Jr 35,57,159, 343		
	(McGehee,Ark; Pres The McGehee Bank)		
1916-	Bowman, Frances W.Walker 57,35,162, (343)		
	(McGehee,Arkansas.)		
1939-	Bowman, Alice Ann 57,162 453		
	(McGehee,Arkansas.)		
1942-	Bowman, Samuel Lee, 3rd 57,162, 454		
	(McGehee,Arkansas.)		
1948-	Bowman, William Walker 57,162, 455		
	(McGehee, Arkansas.)		
1907-	Bowman, Edgar Gherman 35,159, 342		
	(Last address was in the Army stationed in Germany.)		
1894-	Bowman, Hinkle Jordan 35,57,163,164, 344		
	(711 Cape Road, Jackson,Mo; Gas & Oil Operator.)		
1894-	Bowman, Lillian Alma Pape 35,74,164, (344)		
	(711 Cape Road, Jackson,Missouri.)		

Born-Died	-B-	Pages	
1916-	Bowman, Helen Louise	57,164,	ord No. 6.
	(711 Cape Road, Jackson, Missouri)		456
1896-	Bowman, Richard Earl	35,57,163,165,	
	(P.O. Box 87, Jackson, Missouri- Accountant.)		45
1896-	Bowman, Myrtle Cramer	35,57,165,	
	(P.O. Box 87, Jackson, Missouri.)		
1914-	Bowman, James Wilson	58,76,165,166,	
	(235 Elmwood Ave, Jackson, Mo- School Teacher.)		
1906-	Bowman, Edna Ruth Davis	58,76,166,	(4
	(235 Elmwood Ave, Jackson, Missouri)		
1939-	Bowman, James Wilson 2nd	76,166,	575
	(235 Elmwood Ave, Jackson, Mo- Hi-School Student)		
1943-	Bowman, Edna Ann	76,166,	576
	(235 Elmwood Ave, Jackson, Mo-Pupil in Grade School)		
1901-	Bowman, Charles Wells	36,174,175,	348
	(Address unknown, last address St Louis, Mo.)		
1900-	Bowman, Fern Marie Scott	36,175,	(348)
	(316 Benton St, Sikeston, Missouri.) Secretary.		
?	Bowman, Gale Townsend	175,	(348)
1903-	Bowman, Milton Paul	36,174,176,	349
	(1414-A E DeSoto Ave, St Louis 7, Missouri.)		
1911-	Bowman, Velma Mary Chilton	36,176,	(349)
	(1414 -A E DeSoto Ave, St Louis 7, Missouri.)		
1907-	Bowman, Benjamin Lee, Sr	37,59,178,180,	351
	(1504 So. College St, Brady, Texas.) Wholesale Grocer)		
1911-	Bowman, Bernice Irene Haile	37,59,180,	(351)
	(1504 So. College Ave, Brady, Texas.)		
1929-	Bowman, Benjamin Lee, Jr	59,78,180,181-A,	465
	(2301 Guadalupe St, San Angelo, Texas-Student in Texas University, Austin, Texas)		
1937-	Bowman, Sharon Haye Harwood	59,78,181-A,	(465)
	(2301 Guadalupe St, San Angelo, Texas.)		
1956-	Bowman, Barry Lee	78,181-A,	586½
	(2301 Guadalupe St, San Angelo, Texas.)		
1909-	Bowman, Em Harlan	37,59,178,182,183,	352
	(2708 Birchill Road South, Fort Worth, 5 Texas.) (Ocupation: Accountant.)		
1921-	Bowman, Neva Catherine Cox	37,59,	(352)
	(2708 Birchill Road, So. Ft Worth, Texas 7)		
1944-	Bowman, Joe Thomas	59,183,	467
	(2708 Birchill Road So, Fort Worth 7, Texas.)		
1931-	Bowman, Mary Louise Jones	59,182,	(352)
1903-	Bowman, Major James D	37,60,186,187,	354
	(Retired Major U.S. Air Force, Business Representative Bartenders & Culinary Workers Union No. 340, San Mateo, California.) (Residence Address: 2325 Middlefield Rd, Mt View, Cal.)		
1903-	Bowman, Catherine Anne Dodge	37,60,187,	(354)
	(2325 Middlefield Road, Mt View, California.)		
1943-	Bowman, Patricia Ann	60,187,	472
	(2325 Middlefield Road, Mt View, Calif.)		
1906-	Bowman, Wilbur J	37,60,186,190,	356
	(2028 Federal Ave, Seattle, Wash.) Co-Owner in the Taxi Business.)		
1906-	Bowman, Mary Catherine Gubbins	37,60,190,	(356)
	(2028 Federal Ave, Seattle, Washington.)		
1937-	Bowman, Mary Catherine	61,190,	474
	(2028 Federal Ave, Seattle, Washington.) (Studying to be a Nun. & School Teacher St Vincient Convent, Seattle, Wash.)		

Born-Died	-B-	-Pages-	Record No.
1939-	Bowman, W. John Joseph (Seattle, Wash, In Seminary studying to become a Priest.)	61,190	475
1942-	Bowman, Margaret Mary (2028 Federal Ave, Seattle, Wash.)	61,190	477
1940-	Bowman, L. James Joseph (2028 Federal Ave, Seattle, Washington.)	61,190,	476
1946-	Bowman, Robert Joseph (2028 Federal Ave, Seattle, Washington.)	61,190,	478
1914-	Bowman, Woodrow W, (294 Tennessee Lane, Palo Alto, California.) (Manager Personnel Department, Sperry Division of General Mills, Inc-San Francisco, California.)	38,61,186,191,	357
1915-	Bowman, Billie Harrison (294 Tennessee Lane, Palo Alto, California.)	38,61,194,	(357)
1938-	Bowman, Joan Elizabeth (294 Tennessee Lane, Palo Alto, California.)	61,191,	479
1874-	Bowman, John Jasper (452 N.Missouri Ave, Liberty, Missouri.) Retired Banker. (See Biography page 41.)	23,40,Bio'41,	245
1876-1953	Bowman, Betty Hill Dec'	23,40,	(245)
1914-	Bowman, Georgia Bessie (452 N.Missouri Ave, Liberty, Missouri.)	40,	371
1886-	Bowman, Thomas DeWitt (32 Wall St, Wellesley, Mass; Retired Member of the U.S. State Department, Served as U.S. Consular General, see Biography page 43.)	23,40,Bio'43,	249
1886-	Bowman, Lillian Clyde Parker (32 Wall St, Wellesley, Massachusetts)	23,40,	(249)
1917-	Bowman, Thomas Parker (25 Hendrie Ave, Riverside, Conn, Engineering Department, Ralph M. Parsons Construction Co, of New York, N.Y.)	40,65,	372
1921-	Bowman, Sheila Goodall Fraser (25 Hendrie Ave, Riverside, Conn.)	40,65,	(372)
1944-	Bowman, Thomas Alexander DeWitt (Tad) (25 Hendrie Ave, Riverside, Conn.)	65,	501
1952-	Bowman, Grant Fraser (25 Hendrie Ave, Riverside, Conn,)	65,	502
1954-	Bowman, David Parker	65,	503
1877-1891	Bowman, Connie Irene Dec'	23,	246
1879-1898	Bowman, Myrta May Dec'	23,	247
1887-1888	Bowman, Orren Clyde Dec'	23,	248
1892-	Bellamy, Ruth Bowman (Smythe) (2801 Olympic Drive, Bakersfield, California.) (A Practical Nurse.)	138,147,150,34,55,	336
1887-	Bowman, Dr. Paul Haynes (Retired President of Bridgewater (Va) College; Bridgewater, Virginia 1919-1946) Res: Timberville, Virginia)	26,44,	273
1914-	Bowman, Paul Hoover	44,66,	375
1920-	Bowman, John Evans	44,67,	376

Born-Died	-C-	Pages	Record No.
1916-	Coates, Margaret Bowman	58,77,165,167,	458
	(Marion Street,RFD#2, Sikeston,Missouri)Teacher.		
1909-	Coates, Hubert Harlice	77,58,167	(458)
	(Marion Street,RFD#2, Sikeston,Missouri)		
1939-	Coates, Margaret Ann	77,167,	577
	(Marion Street,RFD#2,Sikeston,Mo;Hi-School Student.)		
1945-	Coates, Emma Joe	77,167,	578
	(Marion Street,RFD#2,Sikeston,Mo, Grade School)		

-D-

Born-Died		Pages	Record No.
1917-	Dixon, Adagene Bowman	51,71,121,123,	427
	(858 N-E 97th St,Miami,Florida.)		
1920-	Dixon, Guy Edwin,Jr	51,71,123,	(427)
	(858 N-E 97th St,Miami,Florida; Inventor & Pres. The Panelfold Door Co,Inc also was Captain Eastern Air Lines.)		
1939-	Dixon, Margot Elizabeth	71,123,	539
	(858 N-E 97th St,Miami,Florida.)		
1946,	Dixon, Guy Edwin,3rd	71,123,	540
	(858 N-E 97th St,Miami,Florida.)		
1905-	Duncan, Ray S	36,58,169,	(346)
	(2405 Terry Hill,Cape Girardeau,Missouri.) Division Sales Representative for The Ralston-Purina Co,St Louis,Mo.)		
1900-	Duncan, Anice Lilyan Bowman	36,58,163,169,	346
	(2405 Terry Hill,Cape Girardeau,Missouri.)		
1935-	Duncan, Ray Bowman	58,169,	460

Born-Died   -B-   -Pages-   Record No.

1939-   Bowman, W. John Joseph   61,190   475
            (Seattle, Wash, In Seminary studying to become a Priest.)
1942-   Bowman, Margaret Mary   61,190   477
            (2028 Federal Ave, Seattle, Wash.)
1940-   Bowman, L. James Joseph   61,190,   476
            (2028 Federal Ave, Seattle, Washington.)
1946-   Bowman, Robert Joseph   61,190,   478
            (2028 Federal Ave, Seattle, Washington.)
1914-   Bowman, Woodrow W,   38,61,186,191,   357
            (294 Tennessee Lane, Palo Alto, California.)
            (Manager Personnel Department, Sperry Division
                of General Mills, Inc-San Francisco, California.)
1915-   Bowman, Billie Harrison   38,61,194,   (357)
            (294 Tennessee Lane, Palo Alto, California.)
1938-   Bowman, Joan Elizabeth   61,191,   479
            (294 Tennessee Lane, Palo Alto, California.)
1874-   Bowman, John Jasper   23,40,Bio'41,   245
            (452 N. Missouri Ave, Liberty, Missouri.)
            Retired Banker. (See Biography page 41.)
1876-1953   Bowman, Betty Hill Dec'   23,40,   (245)
1914-   Bowman, Georgia Bessie   40,   371
            (452 N. Missouri Ave, Liberty, Missouri.)
1886-   Bowman, Thomas DeWitt   23,40,Bio'43,   249
            (32 Wall St, Wellesley, Mass; Retired Member of
                the U.S. State Department, Served as U.S. Consular
                General, see Biography page 43.)
1886-   Bowman, Lillian Clyde Parker   23,40,   (249)
            (32 Wall St, Wellesley, Massachusetts)
1917-   Bowman, Thomas Parker   40,65,   372
            (25 Hendrie Ave, Riverside, Conn, Engineering
                Department, Ralph M. Parsons Construction Co, of
                New York, N.Y.)
1921-   Bowman, Sheila Goodall Fraser   40,65,   (372)
            (25 Hendrie Ave, Riverside, Conn.)
1944-   Bowman, Thomas Alexander DeWitt (Tad) 65,   501
            (25 Hendrie Ave, Riverside, Conn.)
1952-   Bowman, Grant Fraser   65,   502
            (25 Hendrie Ave, Riverside, Conn,)
1954-   Bowman, David Parker   65,   503
1877-1891   Bowman, Connie Irene Dec'   23,   246
1879-1898   Bowman, Myrta May   Dec'   23,   247
1887-1888   Bowman, Orren Clyde Dec'   23,   248

1892-   Bellamy, Ruth Bowman (Smythe)   138,147,150,34,55,   336
            (2801 Olympic Drive, Bakersfield, California.)
            (A Practical Nurse.)

1887-   Bowman, Dr. Paul Haynes   26,44,   273
            (Retired President of Bridgewater (Va)College;
            Bridgewater, Virginia 1919-1946) Res: Timberville, Virginia)
1914-   Bowman, Paul Hoover   44,66,   375
1920-   Bowman, John Evans   44,67,   376

Born-Died	-C-	Pages	Record No.
1916-	Coates, Margaret Bowman	58,77,165,167,	458
	(Marion Street,RFD#2, Sikeston,Missouri)Teacher.		
1909-	Coates, Hubert Harlice	77,58,167	(458)
	(Marion Street,RFD#2, Sikeston,Missouri)		
1939-	Coates, Margaret Ann	77,167,	577
	(Marion Street,RFD#2,Sikeston,Mo;Hi-School Student.)		
1945-	Coates, Emma Joe	77,167,	578
	(Marion Street,RFD#2,Sikeston,Mo, Grade School)		

-D-

Born-Died		Pages	Record No.
1917-	Dixon, Adagene Bowman	51,71,121,123,	427
	(858 N-E 97th St,Miami,Florida.)		
1920-	Dixon, Guy Edwin,Jr	51,71,123,	(427)
	(858 N-E 97th St,Miami,Florida; Inventor & Pres. The Panelfold Door Co,Inc also was Captain Eastern Air Lines.)		
1939-	Dixon, Margot Elizabeth	71,123,	539
	(858 N-E 97th St,Miami,Florida.)		
1946,	Dixon, Guy Edwin,3rd	71,123,	540
	(858 N-E 97th St,Miami,Florida.)		
1905-	Duncan, Ray S	36,58,169,	(346)
	(2405 Terry Hill,Cape Girardeau,Missouri.) Division Sales Representative for The Ralston-Purina Co,St Louis,Mo.)		
1900-	Duncan, Anice Lilyan Bowman	36,58,163,169,	346
	(2405 Terry Hill,Cape Girardeau,Missouri.)		
1935-	Duncan, Ray Bowman	58,169,	460

Born-Died	-E-	Pages	Record No.
1868-1940	Evans, George Arthur Dec'	34,56,153,	(337)
1924-	Evans, Charles Arthur	56,153,154,	449
	(3805 Parkway Drive, Shrevesport, Louisiana; Chief Accountant for Mid-West Dairy Products Co, "Golden Royal" Subsidiary of The City Products Corp, of Chicago, Illinois.)		
1928-	Evans, Helen Laclede Nichols	56,154,	(449)
	(3805 Parkway Drive, Shrevesport, Louisiana; Teacher in a Private School in Shrevesport.)		
1893-	Evans, Golden V Bowman (White)	34,56,139,151,153,	337
	(Fannetta Street, Dexter, Missouri.		

	-F-		
1926-	Fox, Jerry Gene	68,110,	525
	(Kansas City, Missouri) 10004 Crane Road,		
1892-	Fox, Roy	50,68,110,	(419)
	(Jackson, Mo, RFD #1,		
1909-	Farmer, Kathleen Forde	51,69,116,118,	423
	(505 E.Cypress St, Charleston, Missouri.)		
1902-	Farmer, Burnice Anderson	51,69,116,118,	(423)
	(505 E.Cypress St, Charleston, Mo; With Buckner-Ragsdale Stores.)		
1933-	Farmer, Joseph Lyman	70,118,	532
	(Presently with Armed forces in Germany-permanently address him 505 E.Cypress St, Charleston, Missouri.)		
1915-	Fuchs, Elizabeth V Bowman	51,70,121,122,	426
	(Sikeston, Missouri)		
1910-	Fuchs, Narcisse Edward, Sr		
	(Sikeston, Mo: Owner & Mgr SemO Motor Co "Cadillac" Agency.)		
1943-	Fuchs, Narcisse Edward, Jr	70,122,	535
	(Sikeston, Missouri)		
1946-	Fuchs, Joseph Paul	70,122,	536
	(Sikeston, Missouri.)		
1948-	Fuchs, Robert Bowman	70,122,	537
	(Sikeston, Missouri.)		
1952-	Fuchs, John William	70,122,	538
	(Sikeston, Missouri.)		
1907-	Fox, Bessie Elizabeth Portis	50,68,108,110,	419
	(R.F.D.#1 Jackson, Missouri.)		

-G-

Born-Died		Pages	Record No.
1903-	Goodwin, Myrtle Marguerite Bowman, (710 E.Main St, Jackson, Missouri) A Home Maker.	36,58,163,170,	347
1902-	Goodwin, Robert Bryce (710 E.Main St, Jackson, Mo; Circuit Clerk of Cape Girardeau County.)	36,58,163,170,	(347)
1925-	Goodwin, Robert Bryce, 2nd (515th 3rd Street, Chaffee, Missouri. Athletic Director & Coach Chaffee High School.)	58,77,170,171,	461
1928-	Goodwin, James Lee (2009 Seminary St, Alton, Illinois; Instructor in English & History, Western Military Academy.)	58,77,170,172,	462
1927-	Goodwin, Mary Ernest Clack (2009 Seminary St, Alton, Ill.)	58,77,170,172,	(462)
1951-	Goodwin, James Lee, 2nd (2009 Seminary St, Alton, Ill.)	78,172,	582
1953-	Goodwin, Cathryne Lane (2009 Seminary St, Alton, Ill.)	78,172,	583
1954,	Goodwin, Thomas Lane (2009 Seminary St, Alton, Ill.)	78,173,	584
1956-	Goodwin, Kimberly Ann (2009 Seminary St, Alton, Ill.)	78,173,	584½
1929-	Goodwin, Lane Alden (2009 Seminary St, Alton, Ill; Physical Educational Director, and Coach, Western Military Academy.)	58,77,170,173,	463
1928-	Goodwin, 2nd, Carol Ann Dunn, (515th 3rd Street, Chaffee, Missouri.)	58,77,171,	(461)
1955-	Goodwin, Teresa Ann (515th 3rd Street, Chaffee, Missouri.)	77,171,	581
1934-	Goodwin, Linda Beebe (2009 Seminary St, Alton, Ill)	78,173,	(463)
1911-	Griffith, Margaret Dysart Bowman Eudora, Arkansas.	54,73,140,141,	442
1908-	Griffith, Charles Jefferson, Jr (Eudora, Ark, Secretary & General Manager of The Dermott Grocer & Commission Co.)	54,73,141,	(442)
1937-	Griffith, Charles Jefferson, 3rd (Eudora, Ark; Student in Banking & Finance in Davidson College, Davidson, N.C.)	74,141,	558
1941-	Griffith, Curtis Burette (Eudora, Arkansas.) Student.	74,	559

Born-Died	- H -	Pages	Record No.
1902-	Heady, Jewell D Portis (40 Lynne Drive, Apt 3, Daly City, California.)	50,68,109,108,	418
1900-	Heady, Emmett	50,68,109,	(418)
1925-	Heady, Ronald Lee (5251 Broadway Ave, St Louis, Mo.)	68,109,	524
1920-	Heady, Robert E (330 Nowland Ave, Peoria, Illinois)	68,109,	523
1899-1944	Hulick, Dr. Lester Paul Dec (Practiced in Mansfield, Illinois)	33,53,136,	(331)
1903-	Hulick, Mildred Rebecca Bowman (Present address 1025 Noel Drive, Apt A, Menlo Park, California. There while son Carl is in Stanford University.)	33,53,115,136,	331
1929-	Hulick, Robert Bowman (Present address: 243 Collan St, Evanston, Ill, as Junior, as a Law Student Illinois University.)	54,136,	438
1935-	Hulick, Carl Webster (Present address: 1025 Noel Drive, Apt A, Menlo Park, California.) Senior in Stanford, University.	54,136,	439
1915-	Howard, Cap't Robert W (Present Address: Stationed at Elgin Air Base, Fort Walton, Florida.)	53,73,132,	(433)
1918-	Howard, Margaret Emily Bowman (Present Address with husband at Elgin Air Base, Fort Walton, Florida.)	53,73,131,	433
1954-	Howard, Margaret Emily (Present Address at Elgin Air Base, Fort Walton, Florida with parents.)	53,73,132,	555
1906-	Higgins, Ted (3026 Highland Ave, Abilene, Texas; Mgr, Meads Bakery, & Dottie Lee Bakery.)	35,56,160,	(341)
1906-	Higgins, Norma Lcuese (3026 Highland Ave, Abilene, Texas.)	35,56,159,160,	341
1919-	Harvey, James Leo	37,59,184,	(353)
1919-	Harvey, Adelaide Bowman (P.O.Box 855, Brady, Texas.)	37,59,178,184,185,353	
1940-	Harvey, Jan Iris (P.O.Box 855, Brady, Texas.)	59,184,	468
1945-	Harvey, James Michael (P.O.Box 855, Brady, Texas.)	60,184,	469
1947-	Harvey, Linda Sue (P.O.Box 855, Brady, Texas.)	60,185,	470
1904-	Hallahan, Lillie B.Bowman (1633 First Street, Atwater, California.)	37,60,186,189,	355
1905-	Hallahan, Thomas Lawrence (P.O.Box 631, Atwater, Calif; Co-Owner Atwater Meat Company, (Wholesale).	37,60,186,189,	(355)
1931-	Hallahan, Carole Jean, (1633 First St, Atwater, California.) TEACHER,	60,189,	473
1910-	Hunter, David (Johnson City, Illinois.)	38,62,200,	(361)
1912-	Hunter, Anna Abernathy (Johnson City, Illinois.)	38,62,193,200,	361
1935-	Hunter, Diane Lee (Johnson City, Illinois.)	62,200,	482
1937-	Hunter, Judith Rae (Johnson City, Illinois.)	62,200,	483

Born-Died	- H -	Pages	Record No.
1922-	Hackney, John H	39,63, 103,	(364)
	(8705 Wickham Street, Berkley 21,Missouri.)		
	Owner Laundry & Cleaning Establishment.)		
1921-	Hackney, Nettie Jane Abernathy	39,63,193,203,	364
	(8705 Wickham St,Berkley 21,Missouri.)		
1947-	Hackney, John H,Jr	63,203,	488
	(8705 Wickham St,Berkley 21,Missouri.)		
1949-	Hackney, Thomas Kelley	63,203,	489
	(8705 Wickham St,Berkley 21,Missouri.)		
1951-	Hackney, Sally Ann	63,203,	490

- J -

1864-1937	Jordan, Thomas Joseph Dec'	20,34, 156,	(220)
1866-1948	Jordan, Nettie Bowman Dec'	20,34,102,156,	220
	(Lived at 4615 N.Lookout St,Little Rock,Ark for many years.)		
1892-	Jordan, Pauline	34,156,	338
	(Address: 4615 N.Lookout Ave,Little Rock,Aranasas)		
1899-1900	Jordan, Maple Ford,Dec'	34,156,	340
1933-	Jones, Roy	64,81,	(494)
	(St Louis,Mo.)		
1933-	Jones, Alberta Marie Warner	64,81,	494
	(St Louis,Mo.)		
1955- ?	Jones,Bryan Douglas Dec'	81,	607
1895-	Jackson, Fred	38,(Has Restaurant)	(360)
	(R.F.D.#1, Trussville,Alabama.) 77th & 1st St,Birmingham.		
1906-	Jackson,Geraldine Abernathy	38, Alabama.	360
	(R.F.D.#1, Trussville,Alabama.)		
1925-	Johnson, Rebecca Gene Bowman	45,67,	378

-K-

1917-	Koons, Grace Bowman	44,67,	376

- L -

1901-	Limbaugh, Melvin Emogene Bowman	32,115,135,	330
	(411 Tanner St,Sikeston,Missouri.)		
1902-	Limbaugh, Milam Laban	32,135,	(330)
	(411 Tanner St,Sikeston,Mo;Owner & Mgr Limbaugh Auto Co.)		

Born-Died	- M -	Pages	Record No.
1894-	Meek, Geraldine Jordan (5302 West Markham St, Little Rock, Arkansas; A Secretary.	34,56,156,	339
1896-1942	Meek, James Holmes Dec'	34,56,157,	(339)
1928-	Miller, Lieut Robert E (2708 Birchill Road, South, Fort Worth, Texas.)	59,78,182-A	(466)
1931-	Miller, Joe Ann (2708 Birchill Road, So. Fort Worth, Texas.)	59,78,182,182-A	466
1954-	Miller, Robert E. Miller, Jr (2708 Birchill Road, So. Fort Worth, Texas.)	78,182-A,	587
1955-	Miller, Richard Alan (2708 Birchill Road, So. Fort Worth, Texas.)	79,182-A,	588
1913-	Miller, Jay William (4007 South Sandusky Drive, Tulsa 5, Oklahoma.) (A Wholesale Drug Salesman, Fox-Vilet Drug Co of Oklahoma City, Okla.)	55,74,144,	(444)
1920-	Miller, Ruth Frances Bowman (4007 So. Sandusky Drive, Tulsa 5, Oklahoma.)	55,74,142,144,	444
1946-	Miller, Jay William, Jr (4007 So. Sandusky Drive, Tulsa 5, Okla.) Student.	74,144,	562
1949-	Miller, Phillip Dale (4007 So. Sandusky Drive, Tulsa 5, Okla.) Student.	74,144,	563
1917-	Massey, Samuel (R.F.D.#1, Trussville, Alabama; Minister & Truck Gardner.	38,62,201,	(362)
1914-	Massey, Melvin Abernathy (R.F.D.#1, Trussville, Alabama.)	38,62,193,201,	362
1938-	Massey, Thomas Herbert (R.F.D.#1, Trussville, Alabama.	62,201,	484
1941-	Massey, Linda Lou (R.F.D.#1, Trussville, Alabama.)	62,201,	485
?	Martin, James (Bessville, Missouri.)	64,81,	(493)
1932-	Martin, Peggy Jean Warner	64,81,	493
? - ?	Martin, Alberta Thomas Dec'	81	602
1949-	Martin, David Gerald (Bessville, Missouri.)	81,	603
1952-	Martin, Patricia Ann (Bessville, Missouri)	81,	604
1953-	Martin, Barbara Ann (Bessville, Missouri)	81,	605
1955-	Martin, Loretta Lynn	81,	606

14.

Born-Died		Pages	Record No.
	- Mc -		
? ?	McNabb, John D, Sr	61,194,	(358)
1920-	McNabb, John D, Jr	61,79,194,196,	480
	(2162 Geyer Ave, St Louis, Missouri)		
1901-	McNabb, Louella Abernathy	38,61,194,195,	358
	(6318 Evergreen Ave, Berkley 21, Missouri.)		
1928-	McNabb, Irene Mufer	79,61,196,	(480)
	(2162 Geyer Ave, St Louis, Missouri.)		
1951-	McNabb, Kevin Charles	79,196,	592
	(2162 Geyer Ave, St Louis, Missouri.)		
1953-	McNabb, Mellissa Lynn	79,196,	593
	(2162 Geyer Ave, St Louis, Missouri.)		

- N -

1900-1937	Noser, Joseph Dec'	38,62,	(359)
1905-1941	Noser, Sarah Lee Abernathy Dec'	38,62,192,197,	359
1918-	Nelson, Audrey H	79,198,	(481)
	(Milstadt, Illinois.)		
1920-	Nelson, Frieda Agness (Peggy Noser) 2 Marriage,		
	(Milstadt, Illinois.)	79,62,198,	481
1943-	Nelson, Joe Lee	80,198,	594
	(Milstadt, Illinois.)		
1950-	Nelson, Vicke Lynn	80,198,	594½
	(Milstadt, Illinois.)		

- O -

- P -

1914-	Price, George Willard	56,76, 158,	(451)
	(309 So. Morrill St, Morrilton, Ark; Office Mgr of The Arkansas Power & Light Co, Morrilton, Ark.)		
1918-	Price, Elizabeth Sue (Betsy) Meek	56,76,157,158,	451
	(309 So. Morrill St, Morilton, Ark.)		
1948-	Price, Mary	76,158,	571
	(309 So. Morrill St, Morilton, Ark.)		
1953-	Price, James Meek	76,158,	572
	(309 So. Morrill St, Morilton, Ark.)		
1873-1929	Portis, Samuel Folsom Dec'	50,108, 31,	(321)
1881-1943	Portis, Irene Baldridge Dec'	31,50,108,	321
1914-	Peterson, Frederick H	75,149,55,	(447)
	(1313 Antonia Drive, Bakersfield, California.) Automobile Salesman.		
1915-	Peterson, Mary Lee Smythe	55,75,147,149,	447
	(1313 Antonia Drive, Bakersfield, California.)		
1947-	Peterson, Sondra Janeane	75,149,	567
	(1313 Antonia Drive, Bakersfield, California.)		
1951-	Peterson, Richard Brent	75,149,	568
	(1313 Antonia Drive, Bakersfield, California.)		

Born-Died		Pages	Record No.
	- R -		
1915-	Rainey, Ray Willie (Dexter,Mo; Fannetta Street,Funeral Director.)	56,152,	(448)
1918-	Rainey, Virginia Lucille White (Dexter,Mo;Embalmer and School Teacher.)	56,151,152,	448

- S -

Born-Died		Pages	Record No.
1892-	Smythe, Ruth Lee Bowman (2801 Olympic Drive,Bakersfield,California.) A Practical Nurse.	34,55,138,147,150,	336
1885-	Shanks, Eula Clippard Bowman (Sikeston,Missouri.)	32,51,114,120,	324
1880-1926	Shanks, William Thomas Dec'	51,120,	(324)
1912-1914	Shanks, William Thomas,Jr Dec'	51,70,	425
1921-1953	Simmons, Frances Emogene Bowman Dec'	52,73,127,130,	432
1923-	Simmons, William Henry,Jr (Sandusky,Ohio; Mgr.J.C.Penny Store.)	52,73,130,	(432)
1943-	Simmons, Sally Ann (Sandusky,Ohio;)	73,130,	554
1925-	Snider, Harold Eugene (Dexter,Missouri,RFD #3,A Farmer.)	56,75,153,155,	(450)
1927-	Snider, Georgia Maurine Evans (A Home-maker) Dexter,Mo.RFD #3.	56;75,153,155,	450
1953-	Snider, Sandy Maurine (Dexter,Mo.RFD#3)	75,155,	569
1955-	Snider, Cheryl Kay (Dexter,Mo; RFD #3,)	76,155,	570
1926-	Smith, Warren Litton (1918 So.19th Street,Abilene,Texas.) Salesman for Dottie Lee Bakery.	76,161,	(452)
1926-	Smith, Mary Louese Higgins (1918 So.19th St,Abilene,Texas.)	57,76,160,161,	452
1944-	Smith, Pamela Ann (1918 So. 19th Street,Abilene,Texas.)	76,161,	573
1946-	Smith, Linda Lou	76,161,	574
1930-	Seyferth, Catherine Anna Bowman (2325 Middlefield Road,Mt View,California.)	69;79;187;188,	471
1929-	Seyferth, Glen Patrick (2325 Middlefield Road,Mt View,California.)	79,188,	(471)
1947-	Seyferth, Catherine Diana (2325 Middlefield Road,Mt View,California.)	79,188;	589
1950-	Seyferth, Susan Elizabeth (2325 Middlefield Road,Mt View,California;)	79,188,	590
1953-	Seyferth, Glen Patrick,Jr (2325 Middlefield Road,Mt View,California.)	79,188,	591
1891-	Smythe, Elmer Lee (Bakersfield,California.)	55,147,	(336)
1920-	Shaler, Patricia Hamilton Bowman (705 W.Park Avenue,State College,Pa.) Home-maker.	40,65,	373
1917-	Shaler, Dr.Amos Johnson D.S.C. (Head Dep't of Metallurgy in Penn State University, State College,Pa.)	40,65;	(373)

Born-Died	- S -	Pages	Record No.
1947-	Shaler, Louise (705-W Park Ave, State College, Pa.)	65,	504
1949-	Shaler, Cynthia Mary (705 W-Park Ave, State College, Pa.)	65,	505
1954-	Shaler, James Lane (705 W-Park Ave, State College, Pa.)	65,	506
? -	Stewart, Glen (Box 517 Walled Lake, Michigan.)	64,	(500)
1934-	Stewart, Sheila Maureen (Bennett) (Box 517, Walled Lake, Michigan.)	64-81,	500
1954-	Stewart, Glenda June (Box 517, Walled Lake, Michigan.)	82,	608
1955-	Stewart, Mildred (Box 517, Walled Lake, Michigan.)	82,	609

- T -

1925-	Timberlake, Virginia Lee Bowman (24 Fabian St, (Annadale Station) Staten Island, N.Y.)	58, 77, 165, 168,	459
1924-	Timberlake, James Henry B (24 Fabian St, (Annadale Station) Staten Island, N.Y.)	58, 77, 168,	(459)
1945-	Timberlake, Sharon Lee (24 Fabian St, (Annadale Station) Staten Island, N.Y.)	77, 168,	579
1948-	Timberlake, James Richard (24 Fabian St, (Annadale Station) Staten Island, N.Y.)	77, 168,	580
1936-	Thilenius, Howard Edward, 2nd (Sikeston, Mo; At present is located with the Armed Forces at Fort Lee, Virginia.)	134-A, 53,	(436)
? -	Taylor, Elmer (P.O. Box 190, Arnold, Missouri.)	40, 64,	(370)
? -	Taylor, Mary Irene Welker (Bennett) (P.O. Box 190, Arnold, Missouri.)	40, 64,	370

- W -

1911-	Wilson, Amy Elizabeth Baldridge (4948 Page Blv'd, St Louis, Missouri.) R.N.	50, 68, 111, 112,	420
1911-	Wilson, Clifford W " "	50, 68, 112,	(420)
1944-	Wilson, Ronald C " "	68, 112,	526
1892-1918	White, James Clarence, Dec'	56, 151,	(337)
1893-	White, Golden Virginia Bowman (Fannetta Street, Dexter, Missouri.)	34, 56, 139, 151, 153,	337
1846-1889	Welker, William H, Dec' (He was buried at the Old Salem Methodist Church Cemetary, 2 miles north of Millerville, Missouri.)	12, 22, Bio! 21-B	(112)
1846-1924	Welker, Sophia Perizade Bowman Dec. (Was burried at Marquand, Missouri.)	12, 22, Bio! 21-B	112

Born-Died	- W -	Pages	Record No
1886-1926	Welker, Samuel S Dec'	22,	239
1867-1920	Welker, Mary A Dec'	22,	240
1869-	Welker, Benjamin Lee	22,39	241
	(4401 Braeburn Road, San Diego, California.)		
? - ?	Welker, George O	22,	242
1867-1914	Welker, Ellen (Nell) Owens Dec'	22, 39,	(242)
? -1906	Welker, William Russell Dec'	22,	243
1892-	Welker, Eugenia	39,	365
	(Was living with her father Benjamin L. Welker at 4401 Braeburn Road, San Diego, California) she was a school teacher many years.		
1894-1918	Welker, Guadeta	39,	366
	(Died at Milford, Utah while teaching in the schools there. Died during the Flu Epedemic.)		
1896-	Welker, Benjamin Lee, Jr	39,	367
	(Teaching in the College at Stockton California)		
1883-	Welker, James F	22,39,	244
	(Living on Star Route out of Glen Allen, Missouri.) James has 3 children, 10 Grand children, and 20 great grand children at this writing, July 1, 1956.)		
1886-1941	Welker, Herscella Anna Pair	22,39	(244)
1914-	Welker, Woodrow William	40,64,	369
	(Star Route, Glen Allen, Missouri.)		
1918-	Welker, Mary Frances Stover	40,64,	(369)
	(Star Route, Glen Allen, Missouri.)		
1940-	Welker, James Lee	64,	498
1952-	Welker, Marilou Kathleen	64,	499
1951-	Wells, Ernest	80,	597
	(Bessville, Missouri)		
1951-	Wells, Thomas (Bessville, Mo)	80,	598
1952-	Wells, Arthur (Bessville, Mo)	80	599
1952-	Wells, Betty Ann (Bessville, Mo)	80	600
1955-	Wells, Kathleen (Bessville, Mo)	80	601
1912-	Warner, Clara P Welker	39,63	368
	(231 So. Spanish St, Cape Girardeau, Mo.)		
1908-	Warner, Albert	39,63,	(368)
	(231 So. Spanish St, Cape Girardeau, Mo.)		
1928-	Warner, Evelyn Maxine Warner	63,80,	491
	(509 Linden Street, Cape Girardeau, Mo.)		
? -	Warner, James Richard (500 Linden St)	63,80,	(491)
1930-	Warner, Cynthia Nadine	63,80,	492
	(Bessville, Missouri.)		
? -	Wells, Murphy Lowell	63,80,	(492)
	(Bessville, Mo.)		
1938-	Warner, Jacquelin Vivian	64,	495
	(231 So. Spanish St, Cape Girardeau, Mo.)		
1946-	Warner, Sharon Faith	64,	496
	(231 So. Spanish St, Cape Girardeau, Mo.)		
1951-	Warner, Kevin Matthew	64,	497
	(231 So. Spanish St, Cape Girardeau, Mo.)		
1953-	Warner, Rita Christine	80,	595
	(509 Linden Ave, Cape Girardeau, Mo.)		
1955-	Warner, Paula Gayle	80,	596
	(509 Linden Ave, Cape Girardeau, Mo.)		

- X. -

- Y. -

1906-	Yates, Lillie Bowman	36,	178,	179,	350
1906-	Yates, Lewis C	36,		179,	(350)

(Residence Hamlin, Texas) Lillie is a Bank Clerk.

Section - A

This part of the History concerns the records of our Ancestry from the early 1700's up to the present date 1956.

We have attempted to record the descendants in chronological order from the time we were able to obtain any information concerning our fore fathers who arrived in this country in the early 1700's.

As you read and observe these records, remember that the oldest descendant we have any record of we begin his record number one (1) and then record each descendant right on down in consecutive numbers to the present time October 1956. The latest recorded is No. 609.

When you find a descendant number near the margin of the sheet, and their name opposite; you will find their children following together with their record number.

We have been unable to ascertain if the family has a Coat of Arms. But we are continually working on any information in search if there is one, and if we find one we will have it printed and mail to each owner of a history.

There will no doubt appear some errors in these records. And if you run across any please notify the historian of such errors that he may get our records all corrected.

B.W. Bowman, Historian
Address: Eudora, Arkansas.

THE BOWMAN GENEALOGY
Compiled By Byron W. Bowman
January 1955

INTRODUCTION

Some forty, or fifty years ago the writer's Great Uncle Thomas Anderson Bowman attempted to gather together and publish the history of his generation, together of his fore fathers. But after considerable effort to obtain suitable information he gave up the idea, due to some failing to co-operate with his efforts.

The writers cousin Joe Bowman of Sikeston, Missouri more than ten years ago started to write up the historical facts, and went to great length to obtain information and records of our early ancestory And to his efforts I am greatly indebted for the wealth of records which he has turned over to me.

The writer has been greatly interested in the family history for a number of years, so during the past year, made up his mind to go into the project of compiling as much of the records as was possible to obtain.

This history will be written mostly of the paternal side of the Bowman families, since there are not too much information available on the maternal sides of the family.

We desired to include as much information in the way of Biography, or Autobiographys as is possible to obtain from our kinsmen. We have asked that they be sent in, but there has not been many complying with my request. If there are any come in after the works have been completed I will be glad to print them and mail to all who have a copy of the history.

It has been my desire to bind this history in loose leaf form, with a three ring binder so new additional sheets can be added as becomes necessary from time to time. I think our binder is neat, and very durable, so the cost is much cheaper than having them bound in book form.

It would have been something out side this world if we had been posible to have had a complete record of every descendant from our fore fathers who came over to this country in 1727 to the present generation. It would have been a great joy for our grandchildren to have reviewed something of the hardships our forefathers experienced in the pioneer days. There will be some experiences offered in some of the Biographies that appear here-in.

The writer will be only too glad to receive additional information from time to time on the expansion of the BOWMAN families, and at least once a year will get out a buletin of changes, or additions that occur during the year. They can then be inserted in your book.

If you find any errors in dates, or ect please drop me a card giving me the desired information, as we would like to keep the history up to date, as near as is posible.

-A-
OUR ANCESTORS

The family name Bowman is of Dutch extraction, coming, as they originally did, to Pennsylvania from Holland, and of whose people the Imperial Encyclopedia and Dictionary says: "The two provinces of Holland rank among the most populous districts of Europe and are distinguished for industry and habits of cleanliness." In this country they acquired the title of Pennsylvania Dutch.

A family legend says that the original head of this now numerous family was Jacob Bowman, Jr who was shot and killed by an Indian while feeding his hogs, the Indian crept up behind a tree, from behind which he fired the fatal shot. This was in Pennsylvania something near two hundred years ago.

A son of this sire was my great-great grandfather, John Bowman, and his wife called "Betsy". To them was born five (5) boys, and four (4) girls. Christian, John, Peter, Daniel, and Benjamin were the boys. Susannah, Fanny, Eve, and Elizabeth were the girls. All four of the girls married in their early twentys, but not much is known about their families. Great, Great Grandfather was a farmer, as most probably his ancestors had been. He fell dead in the yard of apoplexy when about 40 years of age, and when our great grand father, Benjamin was a child.

Great Great grandmother "Betsy" later married a man named Chisholm Griffith, who was very kind to little Benjamin and the other children.

These Pennsylvania Dutch were good, strong, sturdy people, but since our source of information is so limited we will of course have to begin the sketches with a generation further down the line.

On our great grand mothers side we know her parents were named John and Mary Ferguson; that Great grandfather Ferguson was a Scotchman, and that he was killed by lightning as he took refuge from a rainstorm under a tree, when he was not to say an old man. He was well off for that day, owning a large plantation and scores of slaves. We know that our great grandmother, Sophia, was a little child when he was killed. We know that great grandmother Mary Ferguson's maiden name was Hill and that she was of Irish-French-Spanish blood and a woman of fine business qualities. She raised a large family and managed the large estate, including the scores of servants left to her at great grandfathers death. While she kept an overseer to look after the slaves in the fields, yet she personally attended to all the business required to manage a large plantation, and a large body of servants.

Our great grandfather's brothers, our great-great Uncle John was the oldest, and was born in Lancaster County, Pennsylvania; that he was brought to Virginia when six years of age; that he was well off, owning a good farm and a mill; that he was a preacher in the Dunkard church; that his wife, Perizade, was our great grandmothers oldest sister; that they had three sons, and one daughter; Lee, Jack, Joel, and Martha. Which we will mention more of later on.

Christopher another of our great-great Uncles was a Dunkard preacher and had many descendants in Virginia.

Daniel was also a deacon in the same church and also had a large number of descendants in Franklin County, Virginia.

OUR ANCESTORS
(Continued)

Of the great-great Aunts, Susannah married Jacob Peters, Jan 7, 1805; Fanny married John Barnhart, Dec 26, 1808; Eve married Daniel Barnhart, July 30, 1812; Elizabeth married Samuel Montgomery, on Sept 30, 1805, and that it about all we know about our great-great Aunts..

On great grandmothers side there were at least three brothers, Standifer, Edwin and Booker Ferguson. Edwin came to Missouri and later went to Corsican, Texas, from which place our Uncle Thomas A. Bowman had some correspondence with Edwins girls some 75 or 80 years ago, but later on failed to get replies from them at that place. The children were probable all girls. There were some sisters besides our great-great Aunt Perizade and one of them, Bettie Wade, settled in Missouri, but that is about all we know of the family.

Our family has some distinct tendencies. They are: to be preachers by profession, millers by trade, and to raise large families, Almost every branch has one or more preachers and millers. It is also a family noted for industry and longevity. They have not taken to politics and high finance, and be it said to their credit, no one of the name has ever been convicted as a criminal or in any way brought discredit on the good name of the family, as the writer knows of, but for the most part have been old-fashioned Christians and believe that if Mr. Darwin descended from a monkey he is in no way related to our family. They have been mostly Dunkards, who were known as German Baptist, and now known as The Church of the Brethren, and the Missionary Baptist. But you will find many descendants that now belong to most every church, and denomination known.

The Dunkard creed forbade the owning slaves, sueing at the law or going to war. They are not numerous as a denomination, but are a good, honest, faithful, peace-loving body of disciples. They practice triune immersion--dipping the candidate three times, first in the name of the Father, second in the name of the Son, third in the name of the Holy Spirit.

Altogether the family has been proud of its good qualities, and the comparative absence of any vices. While not perfect by any means, they are a pretty good average set of citizens. They have scattered to all parts of the country and everywhere are making good. Some one has said there are a thousand Bowman's in one county in Virginia.

We will start with Jacob Bowman, Sr whom we believe to be the son of Daniel Bowman who arrived on the ship ADVENTURER on October 2, 1727, together with his brother Jacob.
Should there be any person who may read these works, and may know of any other information that would add to, or detract from that which is contained here-in, the writer would appreciate gratefully such information.

BOWMAN GENEALOGY

1. **JACOB BOWMAN, Sr**
   of Lancaster County, Pa.

The name of the father of Jacob, Benjamin, John and Peter Bowman, all of which settled in Rockingham County, Virginia, with the exception of John who went to Franklin County, Virginia, is predicated on the fact that Jacob is listed in the 1790 census of Rockingham County as Jacob, Jr. Nothing further is known about Jacob Bowman, Sr., although he is presumably a descendant, perhaps a son, of either Daniel or Jacob Bowman, both of whom arrived in Philadelphia October 2, 1727 on the ship Adventurer "last from Rotterdam". The ship record gave the name "BOWMAN".

This family is distinct from the English family of the same name and the German family whose name was originally spelled Bauman-Baumann. All three families have had, and presumably still have, representatives in Virginia. The English family settled in eastern Virginia; the others settled in the Shenandoah valley.

Daniel and Jacob Bowman, who came to Philadelphia in 1727, were Hollanders. There is some information that this family was once in England, but lived in Holland for several generations. Daniel and Jacob Bowman were undoubtedly among the group of Hollanders which united with the Church of the Brethren while it was in Holland. They settled in what is now known as Lancaster County, Pennsylvania.

The Church of the Brethren, formerly called Tunkers and Dunkers, was founded at Schwarzenau in the providence of Wittgenstein, Germany, in 1708. The sect was forced to flee from Germany to Holland in 1720 and settled at Westervain in West Freisland. Gradually the whole sect came to Pennsylvania and the church ceased to exist in Europe. Because of their religious tenets, they refused to fight in the Revolutionary War and were forced to flee from Pennsylvania.

The four Bowman brothers who settled in Rockingham County, Virginia were:

2. Jacob, Jr b.   , died in Rockingham County, his widow Susanna Milhouse Bowman m. Isaac Hammer Aug 11, 1795 and removed to Tennessee with five of her seven children. Jacob bought a tract of land in Eastern Tennessee in about 1783. This land was on Boones Creek, Washington County, near Floursville. He is said to have died and to have been buried enroute to his Virginia home after making this purchase. Five of his children later settled in Tennessee, presumably on the land their father had purchased. His widow Susanna who married a Brethren preacher Isaac Hammer of Eastern Tennessee on Aug 11, 1795, (Rockingham County records), ceremony evidently being performed in Rockingham County, Virginia. The Hammers, however settled in Tennessee. The children of Jacob Bowman had probably settled in that area prior to the re-marriage of their mother. Hammer was a prominent leader among the Brethren of the south and likely met Susanna Bowman as she visited among her children. Mr. & Mrs. Hammer were buried in a private cemetery on the farm of J.D. Thomas, more recently owned by his son, Edgar, and located at Indian Ridge Gap on Knob Creek near Johnson City.

Issac Hammer was associated with Michael Krouse and others in organizing the Knob Creek congregation, the earliest of the Brethren congregations in Tennessee. This organization took place in about 1800.

Members of the Jacob Bowman's family migrated to Tennessee from the Broadway community, Rockingham County, Virginia, in about 1785. They probably sojourned for but a short time in Rockingham as they were a part of a movement of Brethren from Pennsylvania and Maryland who settled in the Shenandoah and Roanoke valleys of Virginia and in Eastern Tennessee and western North Carolina.

Among the score or more of Brethren families which settled in Rockingham County from 1780 to 1790 there were two Brethren ministers, Benjamin Bowman, Sr., and his brother, Peter. (Zigler's History of the Brethren, P.43). who were brothers of Jacob, Jr.

3. **Benjamin**, b. Nov 1, 1754, d. Sept. 29, 1829 in Rockingham County, wife Catherine b. Dec 25, 1752, d. March, 21, 1836.

4. **Peter**, b.   d. prob. 1796 in Montgomery County, Virginia, where will of a Peter Bowman was probated, naming wife Sarah and five children.

5. **John**, b. about 1764 in Lancaster County, Pennsylvania, d. 1804 in Franklin County, Virginia, widow Elizabeth (Betsy) married Chisholm Holland Griffith, about June 29, 1811.

The children of Jacob and Susanna Milhouse Bowman were:

6. **David**, b. October 20, 1777, m. December 25, 1799 Catherine Frantz, b. November 9, 1782, granddaughter of Bishop Michael Frantz. They remained in Virginia and had twelve children.

7. **Mary**, b   ,married Samuel Yount. Dr. W.B. Yount. for 18 years president of Bridgewater College, descended from Mary Bowman and Samuel Yount. They lived in Virginia.

8. **Jacob**, b.   ,m.   .He removed to Tennessee with his mother and later settled at what is now Poplar and Bakersville, North Carolina, where he reared a large family. Some of his descendants were men of ability and prominence. The present High School at Bakersville is named in honor of members of this family. It is said that some of his descendants removed to Kentucky.

9. **Daniel**, b.   m. 1780 in Rockingham County, Virginia, to Rebecca Zimmerman. They removed to Tennessee and had six children.

10. **John**, b.   d.   m. Elizabeth Steel. They settled near Floursville, on Bonnes Creek. They had fourteen children. He was buried on the Dee Nale farm near Floursville.

11. **Catherine**, b.   d.   m. John Miller. They lived in Tennessee and had seven children, of whom George Miller, father of John and Joseph, was one. Their daughter, Margaret married Adam Sell.

12. **Joseph**, b. Sept. 26 1784, d. August 12, 1850, m. (1)   Moss, 2 m. Christina Beahn. He was a member of the church of the Brethern, and was known as "Deacon Joe".

3.   **BENJAMIN BOWMAN**
              November 1, 1754
          of Rockingham County, Va.

   The Rev. Benjamin Bowman is mentioned frequently in the History of the Brethren in Virginia. He was born November 1, 1754, probable in Lancaster County, Pennsylvania, and died September 29, 1829 in Rockingham County, Virginia. His wife Catherine was born December 25, 1752 and died March 21, 1836 He removed to Virginia, and lived at Greenmount, Rockingham County. He was the Senior elder of the Brethren Churches north of Harrisonburg from the time of the first division in 1788.

   The children of Benjamin and Catherine Bowman were:

   13. Elizabeth, b. February 12, 1778, m. April 17, 1798 John Byerly (or Birer), d. August 10 1865, age 87, in Washington County, Tennessee.
   14. Samuel, b. September 10, 1779, m. January 3, 1804, Susannah Kratzer, d. November 18, 1861 in Rockingham County.
   15. Daniel, b. March 5, 1781. M. February 8, 1798 Ceny Zimmerman.
   16. Catherine, b. December 11, 1783; m. September 18, 1804, m. Jacob Myers, d. October 17, 1877, age 93.
   17. Benjamin, b. June 28, 1785, m. January 1, 1810, Catherine Wine, b. April 20, 1785. He died April 9, 1872, age 86, at his home near Greenmount, Rockingham County.
   18. John, b. April 24, 1790, m. December 10, 1811, to Susanna Wine, b. September 5, 1787 (sister of Catherine). He died May 30, 1873, age 83 near Harrisonburg, Virginia.
   19. Jacob, b. September 15, 1793. m. Mary   , b. July 6, 1790. He died June 23, 1848.

4.   **PETER BOWMAN**
          of Montgomery County, Va.

   According to the History of the Brethren in Virginia, Peter Bowman was a minister and lived in Rockingham County, Virginia, south of Harrisonburg. He removed to Virginia at the same time as his brother Benjamin. He was not listed as a resident of Rockingham County in the 1790 census and may have removed to Montgomery County, Virginia, before that date. A Peter Bowman's will was probated in Montgomery County May 1796. The will named his wife Sarah and the following children:

   20. Elisha.
   21. Jessee (or Joshua)
   22. William
   23. Emmy
   24. Phebe

5.
John Bowman
of Franklin County Va.

John Bowman, progenitor of the Franklin County Bowmans is said to have been descended from Daniel or Jacob Bowman, who arrived in Philadelphia October 2, 1727 on the ship "Adventurer" John Bowman, with his brothers Jacob, Benjamin, Peter, settled in Rockingham County, Virginia, about 1785 or earlier. John removed to Franklin County. On October 6, 1788, he bought 230 acres on Griffith creek from Martin Ihoy for 30 pounds. In 1789 he was deeded 100 acres in the same locality by his friend Jacob Cradler, consideration "Love and Good Will". Later in 1789, he purchased 116 acres on Little Creek from Robert Mead and in 1792 he bought another parcel of 230 acres from Robert Mead. He died in 1804, leaving to his wife, Elizabeth, his home plantation and 500 Pounds in money. The final accounting of his estate in 1816 showed a total value of $5623.77. His widow remarried on June 29, 1811 to Chrisholm Holland Griffith.

John Bowman was a good farmer, as most probably his ancestors had been. He fell dead in the yard from apoplexy when in middle life around 39 years of age,

Children of John and Elizabeth Bowman were:
(They are not listed in order of birth)

25. Christian, m. prob. Hanna Rinehart of Botetourt County; removed to Floyd County.
26. John, who most probably was the oldest child, m. February 11, 1813 to Perizade Ferguson, dau of John and Mary Ferguson. Mary was the older sister of Benjamin's wife Sophia. John was a miller, and preacher in the Dunkard church.
27. Peter, m. September 3, 1804, to Mary Saunders. He was mentioned in the settlement of the estate of his father but no other record has been found.
28. Susannah, b. January 7, 1805, to Jacob Peters.
29. Daniel, b. October 7, 1795, d. September 28, 1883, m. Catherine Naff, dau. of Jacob Naff, on November 14, 1817, she was b. September 10, 1796, d. April 17, 1878. Both are buried on the original Bowman plantation.
30. Fanny, m. December 26, 1808, to John Barnhart.
31. Eve, m. July 30, 1812, Daniel Barnhart.
32. Elizabeth, m. September 30, 1805, to Samuel Montgomery.
33. Benjamin, b. January 16, 1804., m. July 10, 1826, to Sophia Hill Ferguson, dau. John and Mary Ferguson, he d. in 1873, and Sophia d. April 6, 1896.

6.
DAVID BOWMAN

David Bowman was born October 20, 1777, m. Decemner 25, 1799 to Catherine Frantz, b. November 9, 1782, grand-daughter of Bishop Michael Frantz. They remained in Virginia and had a family of twelve (12) children who were as follows:

34. Jacob, b. April 9, 1801, probably died young.
35. Magdalena, b. January 2, 1803, m. Joel Spitzer and removed to Missouri.
36. Elizabeth, b.   d.   m. John Garber; one of their children was John N. Garber of Harrisonburg, Virginia.

5.

The children of David and Catherine Bowman
(Continued)

6.
37. <u>Catherine</u>. b. November 21, 1806, m. May 15, 1825, (1) Samuel Rhodes. m. (2) David Shirkey; Sally (Acker) was a daughter of the first marriage and Johnston Shirkey a son of the second marriage.
38. <u>Susan</u>. b. December 4, 1808, m. John Showalter, brother of Christian Showalter; W.J. Showalter, of the National Geographic Magazine, was a grand-son of John and Susan.
39. <u>Frances</u>, b. March 16, 1811, m. John Rhodes; David and Frederick Rhodes, of Pleasant Valley, Va were her sons.
40. <u>Hannah</u>, b. May 8, 1813, m. Christian Sites; David Sites and Mary, who married a Bowman, were her children.
41. <u>Annie</u>, b. September 7, 1815, m. _____ Baker; Delilah, her daughter married Henry L. Rhodes.
42. <u>David</u>, b. April 12, 1817, m. Annie Showalter, sister of Christian Showalter; they moved to Missouri and founded a prosperous family in Ray County.
43. <u>Sarah</u>, b. June 20, 1820, m. Christian Showalter, a brother of her sister Susan's husband.
44. <u>Lidia</u>, b. November 14, 1822, m. Philip Depoy, they removed to West Virginia and died there.
45. <u>Joseph</u>, b. November 8, 1827. No further data on him.

8.
JACOB BOWMAN

He went to Tennessee his mother Susanna, later he settled in Poplar, N.C. and in Bakerville, N.C. where he reared a large family. Some were prominent, some moved to Kentucky near Berea, Kentucky. He was a hunter, and pioneer. We have no record of any of his family.

9.
DANIEL BOWMAN

Daniel Bowman of Rockingham County, Virginia. He was the great, great grandfather of Dr. Paul Haynes Bowman, of Timberville, Virginia. He married Rebecca Zimmerman in 1780 before they moved to Washington County, Tennessee and settled on Boone's Creek. They had six children.

The children of Daniel and Rebecca Bowman were:
46. <u>Jacob</u>, b. _____ who m. a _____ Molsbee. He died at 30 years of age.
47. <u>Samuel</u>, b. _____ d. _____ m. Anna Crouch in 1830. He was the great grandfather on Dr. Paul H. Bowmans mother side Was a prominent deacon in the church of The Brethren. His house on Boone's Creek was used as a place of worship by the brethren people. It is a log house and is still standing. It was later the home of George C. Bowman, who was the grand father of Dr. Paul H. Bowman on his mothers side, who was born on February 10, 1832 and died on July 31, 1898. Dr. Paul H. was born in this house.

9. The children of DANIEL & REBECCA BOWMAN
(Continued)

- 48. Daniel, b.   m. Alta Ellis.
- 49. John A. the famous preacher who married Mariah Worthington. He was assassinated near Bluntville, during the Civil War.
- 50. Susannah, b.   d.   m. Solomon Krouse in her first marriage, and James Hinkle in her second marriage.
- 51. Katherine, b.   d.   m. Daniel Geisler.

10.   JOHN   BOWMAN
          of Washington County, Tennessee.

John Bowman of Washington County, Tenn settled near Floursville on Boones Creek, having removed with his mother from Rockingham County, Virginia. He married Elizabeth Steel. They had thirteen (13) children. John was buried on the Dee Hale farm near Floursville, Tenn.

Their children were:
- 52. Benjamin, b.   d.   m. Eliza Gates.
- 53. Jacob, b.   d.   m. Sallie Campbell.
- 54. Samuel, b.   d.   m. Margaret Hale,
- 55. Isaac, b.   d.   m. Agnes Young.
- 56. Madison, b.   d.   m. Isabel Campbell.
- 57. Susan, b.   d.   m. John Klepper.
- 58. Rebecca, b.   d.   m. William Mead.
- 59. Sallie, b.   d.   m. Jacob Zimmerman.
- 60. Daniel, b.   d.   m. Elizabeth Miller.
- 61. Mary, b.   d.   m. Jacob Highsinger.
- 62. Catherine, b.   d.   m. Jacob Klepper.
- 63. John, b.   d.   m. Eliza Miller.
- 64. Joseph, b. Aug 18, d.   m. Mahala Carr.
      1805.

                JOSEPH BOWMAN, Sr.

12. Joseph Bowman, Sr was born September 26, 1784, died August 12, 1850. His first marriage was to a Miss _____ Moss, to whom was born four children; his second marriage was to Christine Beahm to whom six children were born. JOSEPH was known as "DEACON JOE", he was a member of the Church of the Brethren. He was a man of prominence and influence. He was a carpenter, contractor, and builder. He built the brick house on Knob Creek in 1818, and until recently was in the possesion of Dr. Paul Haynes Bowman, of Timberville, Virginia. To this house Deacon Joe brought his second bride. This was the farm house for his 600 acre farm which he had bought principally from the Fain heirs, of John Clark. He maintained The Fain heirs secured it in 1783 by grant from the state of North Carolina before the state of Tennessee was organized, He also built a large brick house on the W.B.Reeves farm, now owned by heirs of John Clark. He maintained a shop in which he employed a number of men 20 to 30 it is said. He made beds, chests, clock cases, ect. Much of the old furniture on Knob Creek, and boones Creek came from his shop. The Brethren on Knob Creek used this home as a place of worship for 30 years.

JOSEPH BOWMAN, Sr.,
(Continued)

12. In all probability the old Knob Creek Congregation was organized in his home - the old brick house still standing and now owned and recently renovated by J. Opie Bacon and his wife, Ruth Bowman Bacon.
He and his second wife are buried in the cemetery at the Knob Creek church. The graves are well marked by stones placed by his son, Joseph, Jr. It is supposed that his first wife was buried in an old private cemetery on the farm which he owned. It is located in what is called the "Grave-yard field". All graves are without markers except plain limestone rock and they have mostly disappeared.

JOSEPH Bowman and his first wife's children were:
65. Susanna, b. April 8, 1807, m. Jim Crouch.
66. John, b. January 9, 1809, M. Salina Broyles.
67. Elizabeth, b. July 9, 1813, M. Henry Bashor.
68. Jacob, d. In infancy.

JOSEPH Bowman and his second wife Christina, and their children were:
69. Mary, b. October 4, 1820, m. Henry Garst.
70. Daniel, b. 1822, m. Catherine Lair his first wife, Margaret Kelly his second wife, and Mary Miller his third wife.
71. Catherine, b. November 18, 1823, m. John Lair.
72. Sarah, b. May 24, 1826, m. Jacob Clark.
73. David, b. May 27, 1828, m. Elizabeth Garst.
74. Joseph, Jr b. September 30, 1832. m. Susanna Arnold on April 12, 1855.

SAMUEL BOWMAN
of Rockingham County, Va.

14. Samuel Bowman was born September 10, 1779; married January 3, 1804 Susanna Kratzer; died in Rockingham County November 18, 1861.

He and Susanna's children were:
75. Joseph, b. November 5, 1804, m. Mary Shaver, d. December 12, 1866 at Middletown, Indiana.
76. Daniel. b. February 7, 1806, m. Barbara Neff, dau of Henry Neff and Barbara Burkholder. Henry Neff was a son of Dr. Jacob Neff who was a son of John Henry Neff who came to America from Switzerland and settled near Mt. Jackson, Virginia. Barbara Burkholder was a daughter of Jacob Burkholder, d. March 12, 1863 in Rockingham County.
77. Annie, b. December 8, 1807, m. Michael Whitemore, d. at Mt. Clinton, Virginia.
78. Simon, b. October 27, 1808, m. Elizabeth Whitemore, d. November 17, 1877 at Mt. Clinton, Virginia.
79. Catherine, b. September 11, 1811 in Botetourt County, Virginia., m. Peter Whitemore, d. October 20, 1880.

SAMUEL BOWMAN
OF Rockingham County, Va.
(Continued from page 7)

14.

80. **Benjamin**, b. January 28, 1814, unmarried, d. May 12, 1893, in Rockingham County, Va.
81. **Hetty**, b. October 16, 1815, M. James Crawford, d. July 30, 1867 at Mt. Clinton, Virginia.
82. **John**, b. November 10, 1817, m. Elizabeth Flick.
83. **Samuel**, b. December 8, 1819, m. Mrs Sallie Shull, d. May 14, 1893, in Rockingham, Va.
84. **William D.** b. November 18, 1821, m. Mary Miller, d. May 15, 1893.
85. **Ephraim**, b. April 30, 1824, d. July 3, 1826.
86. Elizabeth, b. December 3, 1826, m. W.T. Hopkins.

26.

JOHN BOWMAN
of Franklin County, Va.

John Bowman of Franklin County Virginia was born about the year 1790, best we have been able to figure. He married his brother Benjamin's wife Sophia Fergusons oldest sister Perizade on February 11, 1813. He was born in Lancaster County, Pennsylvania; and was brought to Virginia when 6 years old; he was well off owning a good farm, and a mill; he was a preacher in the Dunkard church. They had three sons named, LeRoy, Jack, and Joel J, and a daughter named Martha, who married a Mr. John Sink. The will of John Bowman was entered for probate in Franklin County, September 4, 1871, names his wife Perizade and the following children:

87. **LeRoy H.** b.   d.   Lee as he was commonly called by those who knew him. He went to Illinois in early life, and that is about all we know about him.
88. **Jack F.** b.   d.   m. Elizabeth Boone; he died in Boone County, West Virginia.
89. **Martha**, b.   d.   m. John Sink.
90. **Joel J.** b.   d.   m. Irene Layman; died before 1800.

27.

PETER BOWMAN

Peter Bowman was born about 1786, and probable born in Lancaster County, Pennsylvania, and went with his father and mother to Rockingham County, Virginia; and afterwards settled in Franklin County, Virginia. He married Mary Saunders September 3, 1804. He died before 1850. He was mentioned in his father John's settlement of his estate.

These were their children:
91. **Malinda**, b. 1810.   d.   m.
92. **Elizabeth**, b. 1811,   d.   m.

29. DANIEL BOWMAN
Of Franklin County, Virginia.

Daniel Bowman was born in Rockingham County, October 7, 1795 married Catherine Naff, daughter of Jacob Naff November 14, 1817. Catherine was born September 10, 1796, and died April 7, 1878. Daniel went with his father and mother John Bowman(5) and Elizabeth to Franklin County. Daniel died September 28, 1883 in Franklin County and is buried on the original John Bowman place. He does not appear in the account of the executor of the estate of John Bowman, dated April 1, 1816, but he does appear as a witness, with his mother and brother Christian, to a deed to his brother John, dated February 12, 1811. She was buried with her husband.

The following were their children:

93. Elizabeth (Betsy), b.   d.   m. March 15, 1838, to Abraham Peters.
94. Jacob, b. November 10, 1819, m. Mary Flora (Ferough) the History of Franklin County Marriages on page 42 shows the name as Ferough. They were the grandparents of Mary Elizabeth Bowman, who married Thomas Hardin Bowman ( ).
95. George, b 1824, d.   m. Elizabeth Snyder.
96. William, b. January 7, 1828; d. November 25, 1919, m. February 16, 1854, Mary Graybill, daughter of Henry Graybill of Botetourt County, Virginia and great granddaughter of John Graybill who removed from Pennsylvania to Virginia in 1780.
97. John, b.   d.   m. Sally Flora.
98. Isaac, b. 1827,   m. December 3, 1849 Hannah Naff.
99. David, b. 1833, d.   m Catherine Naff,
100. Daniel, b. Jan 21, 1837, d. March 26, 1923, m. Hanna Flora, March 7, 1865; Hannah d. Oct 23, 1901, age 64-11 months, dau. Isaac & Elizabeth Flora.
101. Rebecca, N, b.   m. John Kensey Sept 19, 1849.
102. Susan, b. 1835, m. Orren Kinsey.

BENJAMIN BOWMAN
1804

Benjamin Bowman was born January 16, 1804, in Franklin County, Virginia, and was the youngest child of his parents. His father fell dead in the yard when Benjamin Lee was a little child, as told elsewhere in these sketches.

The older children were John, the oldest, who married Perizade Ferguson, our great grand mother's oldest sister; Daniel, Christopher and Peter, four girls named Susannah, Fanny, Eve, and Elizabeth, all of which were born before 1800, and the family shows a family of longevity, and we live far down the line since their day.

Our great-great Uncle John was a miller and a preacher, his brother Christopher a preacher, his brother Daniel a deacon, all in the Dunkard church.

When our great grandfather Benjamin was old enough to enter school he could speak only the language of Holland, his parents being what were called Pennsylvania Dutch. In school he was associated with Sophia Hill Ferguson, a sister of his brother John's wife. His brother John was their guardian and they were frequently thrown together till association ripened into love, and love culminated in their marriage July 15, 1826. To them were born the following children: Lucy Ann, May 29, 1827; Elizabeth Mary, June 17, 1829; Charles Chisholm, August 13, 1831; John Otea, August 25, 1833; William Edwin, April 20, 1835; Benjamin LeRoy (Lee), January 31, 1837; James Orin, February 6, 1839; Columbus Carrol, May 27, 1841; Samuel Sterling, October 27, 1843; Sophia Perizade, March 3, 1846, and Thomas Anderson, May 7, 1850, the latter on his mother's 45th birthday. All were born in Franklin County, Virginia, except the three youngest, and of these Sam and Sophia were born at Kanawah Salt Works, opposite Charleston, and Thomas at Cole's Mouth, or Cole Bridge, Kanawah County, Virginia, but now known as St. Albans, West Virginia, though the Virginias were one state at that time.

Of the above children, Charles, John, William, James, and Columbus all died in infancy or childhood, Charles and William dieing on the same day, December 25, 1837, and John nine days later on January 3, 1838. All died of what was then called "quinsy", but now known as diphtheria. Thus was the joyous holiday season turned into one of sadness for the family, and for years to come they dreaded to see Christmas come, especially was this so of our dear great grandmother Sophia.

Great grandfather Benjamin had for a long time been tending his brother John's mill, in fact since he was 18 years old, till about 1842, when he moved over to Kanawah County, in the western part of the state, now West Virginia. From Kanawah County he went to Cabell County, farther west and bordering on the Ohio and Guayandotte rivers, to the mill owned by one Mr. Doosenberry, at or near Bloomingdale, but know known as Barborsville.

From here the family moved by boat in November, 1857, down the Ohio River from Guayondotte to Cairo, Illinois, and up the Mississippi River to Cape Girardeau, Missouri. Only the three younger children now remained at home, though the two older girls, now married, came with their husbands and children at the same time to Missouri and settled in Cape Girardeau County. These sons-in-laws were John Chapman, a cooper by trade, and Thomas Henly, a blacksmith.

BENJAMIN BOWMAN
(Continued)

Benjamin LeRoy (Lee), the oldest living son, at this time preceded them to Missouri, and married Miss Eliza Ford, and it was he who was instrumental in getting all the remainder of the family to emigrate to Missouri, where his father Benjamin had a position in a flour mill at Jackson, Missouri, awaiting him. As he had been brought up at milling from his 10th year.

He and his wife united with the old Bethel Baptist church one and a half miles south of Jackson, of which a Mr. Canterberry was the pastor. Here his children attended with them at many services in this historic old church.

When the war between the states came on the mill at Jackson was burned and he moved to what is now Burfordville to look after the estate of the Daugherty brothers, farm and mill, but the mill had also been burned by Federal soldiers. After a few years he moved up to the Greable mill some miles above Millersville on Whitewater, and from there, after the war, to a house on the Farmington road, thence to Pocahontas, where for years he had charge of the Pocahontas mill owned by S.H.Green and later by John D. Hatcher. Finally, in 1872, he moved to Wilkinson's mill on Apple Creek in Perry County, where, April 18, 1873, he died of pneumonia and was buried in old Apple Creek cemetery at Pocahontas, age 69 years and three months.

He was a Southern man and a Democrat of the old school until the day of his death. Some years before his death, his church having gone down, he and and his wife Sophia united with the Goshen Missionary church near Oak Ridge, with which they were always in hearty sympathy. He was a deacon and very much devoted to his Lord and Master. Though perhaps not without his faults, yet he was a good and true man who enjoyed the esteem of scores of friends, with few or no enemies so far as was known.

We do not know the date of his conversion but he was often heard to say that it was while he was on the night watch at the mill on Cole River in Kanawah County in Virginia, now West Virginia, and he was kneeling beside his mill hopper praying. All at once the grinding of the mill seemed turned into the sweetest music and his soul was full of joy. He went out of the mill and the stars seemed brighter than he had ever seen them; in fact, all nature seemed to rejoice in his salvation. Of course that new music and light and joy was all in his own soul. That is old-fashioned religion, but is is the kind that he actually had. In his younger days he was quite well to do, owning with his wife's share of her estate, large holdings of land and his wife's large number of slaves, but owing to a generous nature he would never refuse to stand security for those who asked him to help them, and to this one thing was due to his loss of a little fortune, so that in his old days he was a poor man. Having been raised under the influence of the Dunkard church, he would not claim any interest in the slaves his wife owned when they were married, but only acted as her overseer of these servants. He was very industrious, a characteristic of the Hollanders; a great gardener, in which he took pride, and was rewarded by having the finest garden in his community.

33. (Continued).   **BENJAMIN BOWMAN**
                      of Franklin County, Virginia.

The following were the children of Benjamin, and Sophia Ferguson Bowman :

* 103. <u>Lucy Ann</u>, b. May 29, 1827 in Franklin County, Va; d. March 1, 1897 at the age of 60 years, 9 months and 2 days; m. John Chapman, (a cooper by trade) on September 28, 1848; they had 3 dau, 5 sons, she and her husband were both buried near Allenville, Missouri.
* 104. <u>Elizabeth Mary</u>, b. June 17, 1829 in Franklin County, Virginia; m. Thomas Henley Dec 23, 1849, he was a blacksmith by trade; They moved to Ohio, and then on to Missouri. They had 5 children. She died on August 7, 1859.
   105. <u>Charles Chisholm</u>, b. August 13, 1831, d. December 25, 1837, at the age of 6 years.
   106. <u>John Otea</u>, b. August 25, 1833, d. January 3, 1838, age 4 years 5 months.
   107. <u>William Edwin</u>, b. April 20, 1835; d. December 25, 1837. age 1 year 8 months.
* 108. <u>Benjamin Leroy (Lee)</u>, b. January 31, 1837, in Franklin County Virginia; d. March 3, 1920 at Sikeston, Mo; m. Eliza Ford October 6, 1856, to which were born 8 sons, and 5 daughters a Biography of him will follow later on in this history.
   109. <u>James Orin</u>, b. February 6, 1839; d. In Infancy.
   110. <u>Columbus Carroll</u>, b. May 27, 1841; d. In Infancy.
* 111. <u>Samuel Sterling</u>, b. October 27, 1843; d. m. Swildac Abernathy, November 5, 1868; he moved to Taft, Florida where he and his wife raised a nice family. His Biography will follow later on in this history.
* 112. <u>Sophia Perizade</u>, b. March 3, 1846, at the Kanawah Salt Works in Virginia near Charleston. d. April 12, m. William H. Welker February 19, 1865; (1888.) To this union there were 7 children born. Her Biography will follow later.
* 113. <u>Thomas Anderson</u>, b. May 7, 1850 on his mothers 45th birthday, at what is known as St Albans, Kanawah County, West Virginia, though the two Virginias were as one at that time. m. Sarah Emma Gholson October 14, 1873, d. March 17, 1915 at Belle, Missouri. buried at Jackson, Missouri.   Biography to follow.

SOPHIA BOWMAN
1805 - 1896

Sophia Hill Ferguson Bowman, beloved wife of Benjamin Bowman, was a woman of strong, sturdy character, with Scotch, Irish, French and Spanish blood in her veins and was the best mother ever a boy had. Her positive religious character impressed her children more than any other religious factor. Many a time she sat and read her bible with tears coursing down her cheeks, that would make one feel as though she had something they did not have. She taught her children to fear God and keep his commandments. In her old and declining years she would often express the wish to go and be with her Lord, and when the summons came in her 91st year she fell asleep as peacefully as a babe falls to sleep in its mother arms.
She died of old age, without a pain or a struggle. Her son Thomas A, has said often the joy he shall have some day when he can join that sainted mother in the city of God.

Her religious experience was rather remarkable. Her conviction of sin was rather the result of her own thoughts and reading the Word of God, and for a long period she prayed and fasted one day each week, hoping thereby to get peace of mind, during which time she read the New Testament through several times. Finally, coming to the end of her own strivings, she laid the book down, exclaiming: "If I am ever saved the Lord will just have to save me, for I can do nothing more." Then all at once her burden was gone and she had rest of soul. This state continued and she began to fear it was an indication that the Holy Spirit had left her and she began to pray as earnestly for her old burden to return, that she might feel that she hated sin as before. This experience she had often been heard to relate. Alas! for some one to instruct her in the way of the Lord more perfectly.

In the vicinity there was no church except a Presbyterian, to whom she went to tell her new found joy. The minister called the session together to receive her into membership, but she said: "You do not baptize people, you only sprinkle them, and my bible teaches me to be baptized." "Very well," said the pastor, I will have a talk with you and explain all that to your satisfaction." Well, he and his elders had many talks with her, but not to the satisfaction of her mind in the least.

One day some two years after a stranger appeared at the door and asked for a night's lodging, saying he was a traveling minister of the Gospel. He was welcomed, and in the course of the conversation said he was a Baptist. So she at once asked him if he would preach to a few neighbors in her house and baptize her and a neighbor woman whose experience was similar to her own. He gladly complied with the request, the neighbors having been informed of the service that evening, and the baptism followed the next day, the minister giving the two thus baptized a certificate of baptism. He proved to be an old-school Baptist and later organized a church in that comunity.
It is not known for sure whether great-great grandmother Ferguson was a member of any church or not, but from the correspondence that Thomas A. Bowman had with some of his Ferguson cousins who were in Texas many years ago he found them to be very decided Methodist, but evidently our great-great grandmother Bowman got her religious ideals from the bible, which she always loved and read till the day of her death. She was born May 7,1805, died Apr 6,1896.

SOPHIA BOWMAN (Continued)
1805-1896

It has been related that once while the family lived on the Daugherty place the following incident occurred: The Daugherty brothers were very offensive to the Federalists and frequent raids were made on the home to try to catch them, for they frequently visited in their home. Once a company of Union soldiers dashed up, surrounded the house and asked my great grandmother Sophia if Fred Daugherty was not in. She informed them truthfully that he had been there but had left the day before, where upon they called her a d--n liar and proceeded to search the house, but not finding Mr. Daugherty, they went away. Another time they came suddenly again and made the same demand, though this time Mr. Daugherty was hiding in a closet upstairs. She answered them thus: "Once before you came and asked me and I told you the truth and you called me an ugly liar; if I tell you the truth again you will not believe me, so you will just have to find out for yourselves." They turned and rode away without searching the house and Mr. Daugherty was not captured.

Thomas Anderson her baby son, were never separated, he living at home except when away at school till the father's death, after which he was married and she made her home with him until her death, April 6, 1896, which occured at Marble Hill, Mo., while on a visit to her oldest living son, Rev. B.L.Bowman, and at her own request she was buried in the cemetery at that place. Her age was 90 years, 10 months and 29 days.

This one more incident which her son Thomas A. related during his life time, and which he said was a source of consolation to him during his life. When he was just a child he was stricken with a severe case of flux and the family physician gave no hope of recovery, but on the contrary said that a few hours would decide the issue, which he feared would be unfavorable. This was early in the evening. He said he would return at midnight and see what the result would be, for he thought by that hour the case would be decided. Great grand mother Sophia retired to her room and prayed most earnestly that her son might recover, provided he would be a good man when he grew up; and that if he would not be such, that he might go then as five of her children had already gone. Then she returned to his couch to watch and when the physician returned at midnight, as he promised, he was greatly surprised to find the turn had come for the better and from that hour his recovery was rapid. He said then and there he wish that all her descendants may meet her some day on the other shore.

She was always an industrious, hard-working woman, a model housekeeper and a fine cook, all of which she taught her daughters. She never was known to speak disparingly of one of her neighbors in her life, as anyone knew, but she was always on the most intimate terms with her neighbors. She seemed to enjoy the most intimate confidence and love of them all.

39.

Frances Bowman married John Rhodes-
Their children were as follows:

114. David,
115. Frederick, of Pleasant Valley, Virginia.

40.
Hannah Bowman married Christian Sites.
Their children were as follows:

116. David of Broadway, Virginia.
117. Mary, who married a Bowman.

41.
Annie Bowman, who married a man by the name of
Baker. Their child was:
118. Deliah who married Henry Rhodes.

47.
Samuel Bowman, who married Anna Crouch in 1830.
He was a Deacon in the Church of the Brethren,
and lived on Boones' Creek in east Tennessee,
He was a prominent Deacon in his church.
Thebchildren of Samuel, and Anna Bowman were:

119. Mary C, who died at the age of 17 years.
120. George C, who married Anna Hylton on February 15th, 1832. He was grand-father of Dr. Paul H. Bowman of Timberville, Virginia.
121. Daniel,
122. Samuel,
123. William B (Squire Bill) He had one child.
124. Robert Gentry, who died at the age of two.
125. Martha, who married Christian Diehl.
126. J.K.Polk, who married (1) Elizabeth Thompson, and who had three (3) children. (2) Hattie Cross they had six (6) children:
127. Catherine,

73.
David Bowman, was born on May 27, 1828, and married Elizabeth Garst.
The following were their children:
There were 9 in all but only 4 reached manhood.
128. Rebecca Ann, married Lane Alfred Pritchett.
129. Daniel, who was an Elder in the church of the Brethren.
130. Peter, of which we have no record.
131. Sallie, we have no records.

74.
Joseph B. Bowman, Jr
Was an Elder in the Church of the Brethren, was born September 30, 1832, and died May 15, 1910.
He married Susanna Arnold on April 12, 1855, she was born June 22, 1830.
The following were their children:
132. Rebecca C, born March 29, 1856, Died September 7, 1938. Married Alfred White on November 27, 1878

133. Emanuel A, was born October 1, 1857, and married Mary Harrington.

16.

74.(Continued) 134. Samuel Joseph,
Born January 18,1861,and Died March 4,1932. He was a dentist,and married Sue Virginia Bowman,who was the daughter of George C. Bowman.They were married on August 26,1886. Sue Virginia was born May 16,1863,and died on March 28,1906. They had seven (7) children by his first marriage.

135. Mary S, was born on July 7,1864,and married to Richard Harrington to whom 5 children were born.

136. John P, Born July 4,1871,and married to Tennie Garst,to whom was born 7 children.

90. Joel J.Bowman,
Married to Irene A.Layman. He died some time before 1866. His will was entered for probate in Franklin County Virginia. They had six children as follows:

137. John Ed,
Born October 1,1839. His wife was named "Betty". He lived to reach beyond the 75th year.

138. Palmyra I, Born 1840,and married a Mr. Peters.

139. Frances P, was born in 1842,and married a Mr.Barnhart.

140. David L. was born in 1844 and lived at Devil's Lake,North Dakota. Was a preacher in the Church of the Brethren.

141. Martha A. was born in 1846,and married a Mr. Peters.

142. Daniel A. Born in 1848 resided at Calico Rock, Virginia.

94. Jacob Bowman,
Was born on November 10,1819,and died on July 18,1876. Was married to Mary Ferough (Flora) on August 8,1839. Mary was born on May 24,1822.These folks were grand parents of Mary Elizabeth Bowman who married Thomas Hardin Bowman.

The children of Jacob and Mary Bowman were:

143. Daniel: Born 1840,and married December 5, 1867 to Hannah S.Peters,dau.of David & Nancy (Stover Peters)

144. Jonathan; born June 26,1842 and died July 30, 1869.

145. Martha: Born 1844,and married Jacob Flora.

146. George: Born Nov 20,1847,Died July 4,1919. Married Emily Hildred Akers Feb 10,1870. She was dau of Nathaniel S & Elizabeth Akers

94 Continued.

147. Hannah, born 1849
148. Catherine, who married Owen Flora.
149. Elizabeth: who married Samuel Ikenberry.
150. Samuel: who married Alie Angle.
151. Ellen: Married James Wray, who removed to Kansas.

95.

George Bowman.
Born in 1824, and married Elizabeth Snyder

Their children are as follows:
152. William: Moved to California.
153. David: M: a Miss Layman.
154. Nancy: M: James Wickham.
155. Price: M: _____ Obenchain, and resided on Williamson Road, Roanoke, Virginia.
156. Rosa: M: Charlie Kinzie.
157. Dorus: M: _____? Resided in Trinity, Virginia.
158. Bettie: M: a Mr. Davis.

96.

William Bowman,
Born Jan 7, 1828, Died Nov 25, 1919, age 91 years. M: Mary Graybill dau of Henry Graybill of Botetourt County on Feb 16, 1854. She was great grandaughter of John Graybill who removed from Pennsylvania to Virginia in 1780, and died in 1819.

The children of William & Mary Bowman are:

159. Sarah C, Born Dec 6, 1854, and M: Joel Ray, and removed to Dayton, Ohio.
160. James A. born April 19, 1856, and married a Miss _____ Flora.
161. Martha Ann, B: Mar 11, 1858. M: Charles Saul and removed to Ohio.
162. Rufus O, born Jan 13, 1860, died June 30, 1862.
163. Jonas D. B: Nov 13, 1861, and M: Lucy _____?
164. Thomas Hardin, B: Mar 2, 1864, M: Mary Elizabeth Bowman #302 she was born Oct 22 1875, was daughter of George Bowman #146.
165. Susan Emily, Born July 23, 1866, and M: James Flora of Franklin County, and Roanoke Virginia.
166. Henry Ezra, B: Dec 18, 1868, M: Emma Shelor, and removed to Roanoke, Virginia.
167. George William, born Oct 7, 1871. M: Evelyn Boone and resided at Wirtz, Franklin County Virginia.
168. Daniel Cary, B: June 7, 1874, died Sept 9, 1933 in Franklin County Va. M: Elizabeth Barnhart, stayed at Boones Mill.

97. John Bowman,
M: Sallie Flora of Franklin County, Virginia and they had nine (9) children as follows:

- 169. Susie, M: David Montcastle.
- 170. Frances, M: Austin Hylton, a brother of C.D.Hylton. Removed to California.
- 171. Abraham, (Moved to Illinois where he married) no other record.
- 172. Catherine, M: Daniel Jackson. She was the mother of Neely Jackson.
- 173. Benjamin, B: Feb 6,1845, M; Julia Henry, resided at Bent Mountain, Floyd County, Virginia.
- 174. Daniel, (No other record).
- 175. Isaac, M: Nancy Peters.
- 176. Eva, M Preston Peters.
- 177. Julie, M: Louis Brubaker.

98. Isaac Bowman.
B: 1827, M: Hannah Naff Dec 3,1849, and removed to Indiana.

Their children were as follows:
- 178. Benjamin,
- 179. George,
- 180. Henry,
- 181. Charles,
- 182. John,
- 183. Jessie,
- 184. A daughter.

99. David Bowman,
Born 1833.
M: Catherine Naff.

Their children were as follows:

- 185. Susan, M: Stephens Peters.
- 186. Joel, M a Miss_____ Pollard.
- 187. David, (1)M: Sarah Naff, Dec 13,1861 a dau. of Abraham & Hannah (Peters) Naff.
(2)M: Mary Elizabeth Austin, called Mollie.

100. Daniel Bowman:
B: Jan 21,1837.
D: Mar 26,1923 at age of 86.
M: Hannah Flora, dau. of Isaac & Elizabeth Flora, on Feb 7,1865.

Their children were as follows:

- 188. Hannah, M: Benjamin Naff,
- 189. J_____ M: Lydia Ikenberry.
- 190. Mary, M: (1) Cephas Naff, (2) Thomas Webster.
- 191. Sallie, M: Thomas Montgomery.
- 192. Betty, M: Douglas Webster.
- 193. Jacob, M: Miss _____ Kinzie.

18-A
Biography of
LUCY ANN CHAPMAN
1827-1897.

Lucy Ann was the oldest of the children of Benjamin and Sophia Bowman. She was born May 29, 1827, just 22 years younger than her mother and her oldest child, Elizabeth Chapman, was born just 22 years after her mother's birth. Elizabeth's oldest son, John Robbins, was born exactly 22 years later; and his first born another 22 years later, making five generations of 22 years each.

Lucy Ann married John Chapman September 28, 1848, and to them were born Elizabeth, Gideon, Benjamin, Annie, Tommie, Mollie, John Sam and Freddie. Possibly there were others who died in infancy. Freddie and Tommie died while small boys. Benjamin died of Tuberculosis several years after his marriage, but left no children. Annie married a Mr. Robbins, who abandoned her after a short time and she later married a Mr. McGuire, by whom she left several boys. Mollie who was one of the jolliest girls you ever saw, married a man named Boman, not spelled as ours and not related. He died, leaving three children, and Mollie remarried a German named Metz, a farmer living near Advance, Missouri. Gideon, the oldest boy, and John Sam, the youngest, both married twice and had families.

John Chapman was a cooper by trade. Both he and his wife died at a good old age somewhere in Cape Girardeau County, Missouri, and are buried near Allenville, Missouri.

She was 69 years, 9 months and 2 days old. I have no record of his age, except that he was about 20 years her senior. Lucy was one of these good, motherly women that every body loved. She was known as a very fine cook. She almost always cooked on an open grate fire and her oven bread was the finest ever.

Lucy was very much like her mother Sophia in many respects. She spent much of her time visiting the sick and had quite a reputation as a nurse. She lived a great part of her life in the country where she was known by every one as Aunt Lucy.

June 12, 1956.

Biography of Elizabeth "Betty" Mary Henley.
1829-1859.

The second child born into this family was Elizabeth "Betty" Mary, but always called Betty Mary. She made her appearance in the home on June 17, 1829; grew up to womanhood in Franklin County, Virginia, where she was born. She married Thomas Henley, a blacksmith, December 23, 1849.

They moved over into Ohio and thence to Missouri in 1857. She died August 7, 1859, of childbed fever, leaving her husband and four children, the baby dieing a week after her death. The children were Benjamin, Augusta, Ida and Samuel and the baby.

Mr. Henley and the children made their home with her parents until all the children were grown, when he married again. Ben studied medicine, became a doctor, married and died in early life. Sam became a teacher, I think, and went west in early life and married. He died in Florida, Augusta was married to a Mr. McCullough and had a nice family. One son had a position as private secretary to Congressman Walter L. Hensley at Washington, D.C. The family lived at Marble Hill, Missouri. Ida married John Wiggins, but did not live long afterward. She was never very rugged, but always was afflicted. Her life was sweet, pure, short and good, and it is a joy to know that it has been said that she will have a place with her Master up there.

She urged all those about her, especially her husband, who was not then a Christian, to meet her in heaven. Her remains were laid away in the beautiful cemetery at Jackson, Missouri.

Once when her brother Lee and his father had a spirited discussion on religion, Lee professing to be an infidel, father expressed the fear that Lee would be lost. She said: "No he won't, there are too many of us praying for him."
She did not leave to see it, as she died soon afterward, but her faith was rewarded years later when Lee was converted.

Written by Rev. T. A. Bowman.

100 Continued.	194.	Cleveland, M: Bessie Cummings.
101.		Rebecca Bowman, M: John Kinzie on Sept 19,1849.
		Their children are:
	195.	Orren Kinzie, M: Susan Ann Tench,(Leuch)
	196.	Baxter Kinzie, Died in his teens.
	197.	John William Kinzie,M:Lassie Teel. (Leel)
	198.	Samanthia George Ann Catherine Kinzie M:John Kinzie,
	199.	Achilles,Kinzie,M: Willie Akers.
	200.	Charles Kinzie M:_____
	201.	Eva Kinzie,M_____
	202.	Sue Elizabeth, M_____
103.		Lucy Ann Bowman. B: May 29,1827 Franklin County Virginia. D: March 1,1897, 69 years 9 mo. M: Sept 28,1848 to John Chapman who was born about 1807 ???.Both are burried at Allenville,Missouri.
		Lucy Ann & Johns children are as follows:
	203.	Elizabeth,
	204.	Gideon, Married twice and had families.No other record obtainable.
	205.	Benjamin, Died of T.B. several years after marriage
	206.	Annie, M:(1)a Mr.Robbins, (2) a Mr.McGuire.
	207.	Tommie, Died in Infancy.
	208.	Mollie,M: (1)a Mr.Boman,and left 3 children. (2) a man named Metz a farmer living near Advance, Missouri. (stoddard County)
	209.	John Sam, M: twice and had families. (No other record obtainable.)
	210.	Freddie, Died in Infancy.
104.		Elizabeth Mary Bowman, B: June 17,1829, D:Aug 7,1859,M: Thos Henley Dec 23, 1849.They moved to Ohio,afterwards to Missouri,but they grew up in Franklin County,Virginia.
		Their children follow:
	211.	Benjamin, who was a Doctor M: and died early in life. No other records.
	212	Augusta, M: A Mr._____McCullough. They had a very nice family and lived at Marble Hill,Missouri.
	213.	Ida, M: John Wiggins. Died early in life.
	214.	Samuel, Became a Teacher, married and went west, & Florida afterwards.
	215.	A baby ,(No records otherwise.)

108. Benjamin (LeRoy) Lee Bowman.
B: January 31, 1837 in Franklin County, Virginia.
D: March 3, 1920 in Sikeston, Missouri where he is laid to rest by the side of his wife Eliza Jane. Their resting place is in the Sikeston Mausoleum. He married Eliza Jane Ford October 6, 1856. She was born in Putnam County, Virginia February 21, 1840. She died on June 25, 1930 at Little Rock, Arkansas at the home of her daughter Mrs. Nettie Jordan.

Benjamin Lee & Eliza Jane Bowman were blessed with twelve (12) children as follows:

216. Amy Sophia,
Born: Sept 23, 1857.
D: May 18, 1899.
M: Robert Baldridge,
B: Feb 4, 1934.
D: Dec 11, 1895.
They had 3 children.

217. William Chesley,
B: Sept 27, 1959.
D: April 22, 1950
M: Emma Estes,
B: Feb 1, 1864
D: Jan 5, 1938
They had 10 children.

218. Charles Christopher,
B: Sept 4, 1861.
D: Feb 4, 1906.
M: Martha Emeline Whitener (Bedford)
On October 23, 1833.
B: Feb 14, 1853
D: October 14, 1935.
They had 5 children.

219. Mary Lee,
B: Oct 20, 1863
D: In Infancy.

220. Nettie,
B: June 19, 1866.
D: Feb 4, 1948
M: Thomas Joseph Jordan,
B: March 21, 1864.
D: Sept 1, 1937
M: June 29, 1891.
They had three children.

221. Samuel Lee,
B: Sept 11, 1868.
D: July 6, 1949
M: (1) Annie Gherman, (2) Edna McCloy (Leeper)
B: March 25, 1871. B: April 14, 1880
D: May 18, 1927. M: Feb 22, 1928
First marriage they had three children, and none by the second marriage.

(Continued to next page #21.)

111.

Biography of Samuel Sterling Bowman.
1843-

Samuel Sterling Bowman, the seventh son in succession of Benjamin and Sophia Bowman, was born October 27,1843,at Kanawah Salt Works, opposite Charleston,Kanawah County,Virginia, now West Virginia, and was sugested that he ought to become a doctor; but just at the time of life such things are decided there were squally times surrounding young Samuel, caused by the Civil War, and shouldered a gun and joined the Confederate Army.
When he was about 14 yearsold the family migrated to Missouri, just as the war cloud was rising, and in 1864 he was pressed into the Federal militia, much against his inclination,but being at home on a furlough when General Price made his whirlwind raid through Missouri,he followed up and enlisted in the Eighth Missouri Calvary, Bill Jeffries,Colonel, in command, and was assigned to Captain Stephan Campbell's company. He first smelled powder at Ironton,Missouri., after which that was a daily experience, for he was in thirty skirmishes in his first thirty days of service though he was never scarred.

After a long time he was sent to Richmond,Virginia,parolled and put in a parole camp at Columbus,Georgia,to be exchanged, but General Sherman came along that way and the parole squad was hastened off to Macon,Georgia, given furloughs and turned loose, but the war closed before he reached his old command.

After peace was made he returned to his home and as many of his ancestors had done,and he began to learn how to make flour. He became the peer of any man on that job and after he retired from active milling he retained his interest in the mill at Pocahontas,Missouri., where he had a home. He had another home in Oak Ridge,Mo., but finding the Missouri winters too severe for his advancing years, he moved to Taft,Florida, and spent his last years there.

November 5, 1868, he was married to Miss. Surilda C. Abernathy, who proved to be a helpmate indeed.

They had ten children born to them,four who died in infancy. Robert DeWitt died just as he was reaching manhood and James after he reached his majority. The others were: Mrs.Lou Starrett,whose husband was a farmer living near Neely's Landing, Mo; Mrs. Grace Haldorf, wife of a farmer at Taft,Florida; Rev. Samuel Russell who was a pastor of the Baptist church at Farson, Iowa, and Lyman, who was an engineer and lived at home with his parents. Russell was an expert miller when he entered the ministry

Sam Bowman had perhaps as many friends and as few enemies as any man ever had.
He was an honored and loved Deacon in his church and said that he might have been a preacher if he had "gumption" enough, but as it was he chose the next best trait of his family and became a flour miller. He was always an industrious,hard worker and deserved the quiet retirement of his Florida home, with a competency for his remaining days. His wife proved to be a true and worthy companion,a woman of great energy and with an eye to business,for she always made money on the side with her fowls,pigs,and calves,and was the first of the name, I think, to own an automobile. Her youngest son,Lyman, though already an engineer, went to St Louis and took a course in a school for chauffeurs and soon learned to drive the car well.

The Historian tried to contact relatives in Taft,Florida,but had no results.

MRS SOPHIA WELKER POPE.
1846- 1924.

Sophia Perizade, the tenth child of Benjamin and Sophia Bowman, was born March 3, 1846, at the Kanawah Salt Works in Virginia. As she grew to womanhood she had some serious trouble with her eyes and was practically blind for a long time, though she so far recovered her sight that she was able to perform her household duties, even reading if the print was fairly good.

On February 19, 1865, she was married to William H. Welker, who some time later was converted, and though all his family were Methodists, he united with his wife, to the Baptist church and soon began to preach, showing great earnestness. He won many converts in the years to follow till his death on April 12, 1888, which was very sudden. He had gone to a home of a friend to spend the night, became ill and died in a few hours.

Of his past life he would often say: "What a change His Word can make, turning darkness into day." If he had been a very ungodly man before his conversion, he was surely a very pious one afterward.

The children born to William and Sophia Welker were: Samuel who became a railroad worker at Fornfelt, Missouri; Mary, who married "Bud" Lewis, a farmer at Allenville, Missouri; Ben, who became a telegraph operator and was at one time located at Caliente, Nevada, and who is still living at this writing at 4401 Braeburn Rd, San Diego 16, California, his daughter Eugenia M. Welker now lives with him. George became a farmer living near Blodgett, Mo, but so far have been unable to locate him, if still living; Russell who died in Mexico City, Mexico, August 1, 1906 of small pox; and James who is a deaf mute, who became a shoe worker in a shoe factory at Cape Girardeau, Missouri, and whose wife was also deaf and dumb. James at this writing is still living with his son Woodrow living on Star Route out of Glen Allen, Mo, his wife died in June 1941. James has 3 children, 10 grand children, and 15 great grand-children.

Mrs. Welker remained a widow until after all her children were grown, after which she married Judge M. J. Pope and they lived at Marquand, Missouri. Judge Pope served two terms as Associate Judge from the southern district of Madison County, having been elected on the Democratic ticket over one of the most popular men in the Republican party who had served the county in the State Legislature.

Sophia was naturally a good woman with a strong mind and a bright intellect. She studied the Bible more than most people and was well posted on questions of Biblican knowledge. Her disposition was a cheerful one.

Besides the children mentioned above, four died in infancy and was buried in Old Salem graveyard, where the body of Mr. Welker lies, and a marble shaft to mark the spot was erected by the Oak Ridge Baptist church, of which he was the highly esteemed pastor at the time of his death.

June 12, 1956.

BIOGRAPHY of THOMAS ANDERSON BOWMAN.
1850- 1915

Thomas Anderson Bowman, the youngest of eleven children of Benjamin and Sophia Bowman, was born on May 7,1850, on his mother's 45th birthday, at what is now known as St.Albans, Kanawah County, West Virginia, though the states were one at that time. Later the family moved from Kanawah to Cabell County, at Bloomingdale, on the Guyandotte River, where his father had charge of a mill owned by a Mr.Doosenberry. Here Thomas grew up to be seven and a half years old, learning to swim and fish in the river under the tutelage of his brother Samuel Sterling. Once he caught a fish that weighed 25 pounds and was just as long as the young angler. Of course his big brother had to assist him in landing it.

Small steamboats came up the river and at the mill were a lock and a dam. He could just remember these and the house in which they lived; the big trees, the high river banks; a little creek crossing the road, over which was a bridge; of being very sick once, and of moving to Missouri by boat, down the Ohio river and up the Mississippi to Cape Girardeau, Missouri.

One thing on the trip he especially remembered. At Cincinnati, Ohio the father took all ashore to see, for the first time, a railroad, and his only recollection was to see some houses, to start and run away. That was in November, 1857, and the destination was Jackson, Missouri, where his father Benjamin had a position awaiting him in a mill.

At Jackson young Thomas entered the semi-public school. Half the tuition was paid by public taxes and half by the pupils or their parents. He remembered well the first money he earned, which he used to pay his tuition. That first money was earned for a summer's work for a Mr.Edward Jenkins at twenty five cents (25¢) a day. It was first for dropping corn, then carrying bundles in harvest and for hoeing corn.

Soon those stormy days of the Civil War came on. The rising clouds and muttering thunders foreboded trouble and it was not long until schools were closed, not to open until the four years of struggle ended, and the school terms were exceedingly short and of little real value.

When the war broke out in 1861 the mill was burned, and the family now consisted of ten members, for his sister, "Betty", had died and her husband, Mr.Henley and his four children came to live with the family. Once more they moved to what is now Burfordville, to look after the estate of the Daugherty brothers--Sam and Fred-- who had gone into the Confederate Service. They had a fine stone mill on Whitewater, but it had also been burned by the Federal soldiers. It was so "squally" here that it did not take long for another move, this time to a mill further up on Whitewater and off a main thoroughfare. The mill was owned by a Mr. Greeable, who was away.

The boy got to school by a two or three mile walk for a short term in the winter and worked on the neighboring farms two or three months in the summer until he was 18 years of age, spending the rest of his time hunting and fishing. When he became 18 he began to learn carpentry and while attending a meeting held in the residence of John T.Ford by James Reid and J.P. Bridwell, two Baptist ministers, he was converted and baptized on December 28, 1868

(Next page Continued)

21-D.   (Continued)
Biography of Thomas Anderson Bowman
1850- 1915.

Young Thomas continued his apprenticeship till 1871. Having been licensed to preach in that year, he resolved to enter William Jewell College at Liberty, Missouri, which he did the following September. There were 150 students in the college at that time, 50 of whom were studying for the ministry. He was the first student to enter the school from Southeast Missouri.

Funds were scarce, so he did odd jobs and practiced the most strict economy to remain in school until 1873, when his funds were exhausted entirely. He then secured a school and taught at Orrick, in Ray County, Missouri. It was during this time that his father died, and he returned to his mothers side, who was left alone.

The little country church at New Bethel in Cape Girardeau County, Missouri called him to its pastorate and he was ordained June 14, 1873. On October 14 the same year he was married to Miss Sarah Emma Gholson. To this union were born six children, of whom but two survive, at this writing, John J, the oldest, and Thomas DeWitt, next to the youngest. The others were Connie Irene, who died at Slater, Mo., July 26, 1891, of heart failure cause by St. Vitus Dance, aged 14 years; Myrta May, who died at Fredericktown, Mo, September 28, 1898, age 19; Bessie Beulah, who married John Willis Alexander of Williamsville, Mo.: June 12, 1905, and died at Williamsville, July 27, 1912, age 30; and Orren Clyde, born and died in Steelville, Mo., age two months.

For more than forty years he preached to churches at Jackson, Salem, Steelville, Pacific, Slater, Corder, Chaffee, Owensville, and Belle, in Missouri, besides at quite a number of country churches; he served as Superintendent of the Missouri Baptist Orphans' Home at Pattonville, Mo., near St Louis.

As a side line he also engaged in newspaper work for several years at Fredericktown and Sikeston, Mo. He also published a little book, "Truth in a Nutshell About Baptist," which had a rapid sale and the edition was soon exhausted.

He was fully identified with the denominational work in the state, attending nearly all the sessions of the Missouri Baptist General Association from 1870, when it met at the Second Baptist Church in St Louis on Sixth Street, until a short time before his death.

In the history of the Missouri Baptist General Association by the Rev. W. Pope Yeaman, is the following reference:

"Rev, T.A. Bowman has been mentioned before in these record as an active Secretarial adjunct. He has been associated in such work a greater number of years than any other agent of the General Association. This alone testifies to the high esteem in which he is held by his brethren. His name is inseparable from the Baptist history of Southeast Missouri. There is perhaps not a Baptist in all that quarter of the state that does not know and respect him. Other portions of the state are acquainted with his work and love him for his work's sake."

"This one thing I do" was the watchword of this good man, and that was to preach the Gospel. This he did for over 40 years, celebrating the 40th anniversary of his ordination to the ministry on June 14, 1913. Like Paul, he worked often with his own hands at carpentry, school teaching once for a little while merchandising at newspaper editing, ect., to support and educate his family. He never set a definite salary as a condition of acceptance of a pastorate or other kingdom work.

21-E. (Continued)
Biography of Thomas Anderson Bowman.
1850-1915.

He believed a workman is worthy of his hire, but he also believe that there are fields to be cultivated that could not properly compensate the laborers and in such cases the laborers go into the vinyard and work and trust the rest to the Master.
He kept a complete record of sermons preached, with time, place and text; names and dates of all marriages and baptisms performed and also all money received from all sources for his compensation. The record for these forty years from 1873 to 1913 show the following items:

```
Sermons preached,         5000
Baptisms administered,    727
Couples married,          180
Total receipts,      $ 29,800.00
```

He was a member of Excelsior Masonic Lodge at Jackson, Mo.
He died at Belle, Missouri., March 17, 1915.
The Obituary appearing in the "WORD & WAY" follows:

Today we buried my father at his old home in Jackson, Mo. Others have expressed much-appreciated words of tribute, but I knew him even better than they. A stranger who attended the funeral service said: "That must have been one of the greatest men in the state," and was great--great in his simplicity, great in the faith, great in his earnestness and devotion to the cause he preached, and great in the pure, devoted life of service he lived.

In the midst of our grief we are proud of the heritage he has left us, for we know that his life was one of meakness and gentleness, without guile, hypocricy or deceit, full of good works and service-- a life in which there is nothing to be sorry or ashamed of, but everthing to be proud of. A friend said: "I would rather the things said about me that were said over his body today than to be President of the United States," and the appreciation of his virtues helps to relieve the sting of sorrow.

As pastor, missionary worker, representative of the denominational paper, the Orphans Home and other interests, he has gone up and down the state, in season and out, never faltering or complaining, but doing the work he felt called to do and serving his Master and his brethren. Difficulties and discouragements never halted him, and in all things he was faithful to the end.

With the closing of the year he resigned his last pastorate and expressed the belief that his work was about done. Though seriously ill only a few days, he said he was tired and wanted to rest. He knew he was ready. After a night of suffering, as the morning sun was rising, "God's finger touched him and he slept." As a tired child falls asleep, his spirit entered into that new day of everlasting sunshine to meet his Master whom he had served so long and so faithfully. He "crossed over the river and now rests under the trees."

And so we are proud that we can pay this humble tribute, through our sorrow, for we know that he fought a good fight, he finished the course, he kept the faith, and that a crown was laid up for him.

(This tribute was furnished the historian by John J. Bowman, Bonne Terre, Misouri., dated March 19, 1915.)

113.
(Cont)   21- F.
            Biography of Mrs Sarah Emma Gholson BOWMAN.
                           1850-1918
                    (Wife of Thomas A.Bowman)

           The wife of Rev. T.A.Bowman was Miss Sarah Emma Gholson,
daughter of Felix G.Gholson, of an old Kentucky family, and
Harriett Elizabeth McNeal Gholson, who was born and raised in
Washington County, Missouri.
           Mrs. Bowman was born near Jackson,Mo., April 25, 1850,
where she grew to womanhood. Her father died when she was five
years of age, and her mother died when she was twelve, after which
she lived with the family of Jasper Tooke. She attended the public schools and when grown taught several terms in the schools of
the neighborhood.
           Her parents were Methodists and she attended the services
at the McKendry Chapel and camp ground. She never heard a Baptist
preach until she was grown and never saw anyone baptized until the
day she herself was baptized, along with others at Hubble Creek
Church in 1868, by Rev. John Henry Clark. She had been accustomed
all her life to witnessing the sprinkling of converts and little
children, but when she "played church" with her dolls she always
had them shout and then dipped in a barrel of water for the baptism. Evidently she got her ideas from the New Testament, for
she had always been a Baptist from her earliest recollection.
           She was married to Thomas A.Bowman October 21, 1873, Rev.
James Reid performing the ceremony.
           She became the mother of six children, all of whom died
before her death except John J, the oldest, and Thomas DeWitt, next
to the youngest. There were three boys, and three girls.
           She was an extensive reader, having read most of the popular books of her day; was a great lover of flowers, and showed
some talent for painting but did not cultivate it to any extent.
She did much fancy work, in which she delighted.
           She was very true and faithful in three things: to her
husband, her children and her church. Though never rugged in
health, yet she devoted her life to these things without stint. She
made friends wherever she went, yet never flattered people to gain
their friendship. She was strongly favorable to the Woman's Missionary Society, but took very little stock in Ladies Aids. She was
an anti-suffragist, believing that woman's sphere is in the home.
           After the death of her husband she made her home with her
son, John J, at Bonne Terre, Missouri., and died there April 3, 1918.
           HERE IS A BILL OF SALE of a negro girl sold to Felix
G.Gholson her father.(This is a copy of the original Bill of Sale).

           "I have this day sold at Public sale to Felix G.Gholson he being
the highest bidder a negro girl named Lilly supposed to be eight
or nine years of age for the sum of Six Hundred & five Dollars,
the right whereof is hereby acknowledged, said negro Girl being
one of the slaves which belongd to the Estate, of James Gholson
Dec'd. I do by these presents convey to said Gholson all the
rights and title said Gholson held to said Slave. December 15th,
1853.
                              John C.Metcalf, Administrator.
                              of James Gholson , Died.

108 Continued.

222. James Reed Bowman.
   B: October 21, 1870.
   D:
   M: Lillie B. Lively, August 30, 1892.
   B: September 17, 1873.
   D:
   They have 4 children.

223. Thomas Ford Bowman.
   B: November 6, 1872.
   D: December 27, 1935.
   M: Minnie Van Doren.
   B: September 27, 1872.
   D: April 2, 1953
   (They had two boys.)

224. Lou Ella Bowman.
   B: January 13, 1875.
   D: November 23, 1878.

225. Joseph Maple Bowman.
   B: June 12, 1877.
   D: January 31, 1952.
   M: (1) Lillie Donaldson, (No children)
   B: April 6, 1883.
   D: December 1904.
   Married Sep't 15, 1901.
   M: (2) Minnie I. Brodnax,
   B: June 15, 1882.
   D: November 13, 1955.
   (They had four children.)

226. Wilbur Talley Bowman.
   B: December 22, 1878.
   D: June 29, 1940.
   M: Hattie Donaldson, (Sep't 15, 1901.)
   B: June 6, 1881.
   D:
   (They had four children.)

227. Anna Bowman.
   B: October 20, 1880.
   D: August 1, 1955.
   M: Thomas Alexander Abernathy.
   B: November 11, 1870.
   D: April 6, 1938.
   (They had seven children.)

228. Franklin Bowman.
   B: March 14, 1884.
   D: In Infancy.

SAMUEL STERLING BOWMAN.
   B: October 27, 1843, at the Kanawah Salt Works near Charleston, W.Va.
   D: (No record)
   M: Surilda C. Abernathy on Nov 5, 1868. He retired at Taft, Florida some years ago, where he probably died. Was unable to secure up to date records, or information. They had ten (10) children.

111.(Continued)

22.
The children of Samuel and Surilda Bowman are as follows:
229. _____ NO RECORD.
230. _____ NO RECORD.
231. _____ NO RECORD.
232. _____ NO RECORD.
233. Robert DeWitt Bowman.
(He died just before reaching manhood
234. James Bowman,
Died after reaching manhood.
235. Lou Bowman.
M: a Mr.Starrett, a farmer living near Neelys Landing, Missouri.
236. Grace Bowman. She married a Mr. Haldorf, a farmer at Taft, Florida.
237. Samuel Russell Bowman, was a pastor of a Baptist Church at Farson, Iowa.
238. Lyman Bowman, was an engineer and lived at home with his parents.

112.
SOPHIA PERIZADE BOWMAN.
B: March 3, 1846.
D: February 2, 1924, Bur. Marquand, Mo.
M: (1) William H. Welker,
B: November 20, 1846.
D: April 12, 1889. Bur. Old Salem Meth' Church Cem' 2 mi N. Millerville, Mo
M: (2) Judge. M.J. Pope, who served two terms as Associate Judge Southern Dist of Madison Co, Mo. (No Child)
Sophia & William Welker's children:
239. Samuel S. Welker.
B: 1886.
D: February 2, 1926.
240. Mary A. Welker.
B: November 27, 1867.
D: In the fall of 1920.
241. Benjamin Lee Welker.
B: November 28, 1869.
D: (Still living
242. George O. Welker. NR. at this time)
B: Last report he was
D: living near Blodget,
243. William Russell Welker. Mo.
B: ?
D: August 1, 1906, Mexico City, Mexico.
244. James F. Welker,
B: November 8, 1883.
D:
M: Herscella Anna Pair.
B: November 15, 1886.
D: June 12, 1941.
At this writing 6/1956 JAMES has 3 children, 10 Grand children, and 15 great grandchildren, and nearing his 73rd birthday in November. He lives on Route 2, Glen Allen, Mo.

113.
THOMAS ANDERSON BOWMAN
Born May 7,1850 at Coles Mouth, Kanawah County, West Virginia.
Died March 17, 1915
Married Sarah Emma Gholson
B: April 25,1850.
D: April 3, 1918.
Thomas Anderson and Sarah Emma Bowmans' children are:

245. John Jasper Bowman.
B: August 30,1874. D:
M: Betty Hill,
B: June 16, 1876.
D: September 28, 1953.
They have one child.

246. Connie Irene.
B: September 1,1874.
D: July 26,1891; age 14 years.
(Unmarried)

247. Myrta May Bowman,
B: September 8, 1879.
D: September 28,1898.
(Unmarried)

248. Bessie Beulah Bowman,
B: July 20, 1882.
D: July 27, 1912. Age 30 years.
M: John Willis Alexander of Williamsville, Mo, on June 12,1906

249. Thomas DeWitt Bowman,
B: March 14,1886.
D:
M: July 11,1916 to Lillian Clyde Parker.
B: Aug 16,1886.
They have two children.

250. Orren Clyde Bowman.
B: December 6,1887
D: February 12, 1888.
Died in Steelville, Missouri Age 2 months.

120.
GEORGE C. BOWMAN.
B:
D: July 31,1898.
M: Anna Hylton on February 15, 1832.

George & Anna's children are as follows:
251. William Bowman,
B: October 7, 1861.
D: August 25,1882.

252. Sue Virginia Bowman
B: May 16,1863.
D: March 28,1906.
M: Samuel Joseph Bowman.

120.
Continued from
page 23.   253.   Samuel A. Bowman,
                   B: October 25, 1864.
                   D: March 20, 1920.
                   M: Bonnie Broyles.

            254.   Polk Bowman,
                   B: June 14, 1866.
                   D: October 29, 1887.

            255.   John H. Bowman
                   B: December 22, 1867.
                   D: October 30, 1905. Age 38 years.
                   He became a prominent lawyer.
                   M: Jessie Kirkpatrick.

            256.   J Robert Bowman.
                   B: November 20, 1869.
                   D: January 25, 1909. Age 39 years.
                   M: Julia Keefaver.

            257,   George Bowman.
                   B: January 1, 1872.
                   D: May 21, 1881.
                   Killed in an accident 9 years of age.

            258.   Charley A. Bowman.
                   B: January 21, 1876.
                   D: April 6, 1947.
                   M: Mary White.

            259.   Walter H. Bowman.
                   B: February 8, 1878.
                   D: August , 1949. Age 71-6 mo.

128.   REBECCA ANN BOWMAN.
                    B:
                    D:
                    M: Lane Alfred Pritchett.
                    Have the record of only one child.
            260.   Ruel B. Pritchett of White Pine, Tennessee,
                    is a member and preacher in the Church of
                    the Brethren.

132.   REBECCA C. BOWMAN.
                    B: March 29, 1856.
                    D: September 7, 1938.
                    M: Alfred White on November 27, 1878.

                    The following ten children are Rebecca &
                    Alfred White.
            261.   Minnie B. White
                    B: August 16, 1879.
                    D:
                    (No children.)
            262,   Mary B. White
                    B: November 21, 1881.
                    D:
                    M: Chas A. Bowman on Dec 21, 1912. (3 children)

132.
Continued.

263. Robert White.
B: October 25, 1883
M: Effie Miller
(Had 5 children)

264. Addie White.
B: September 18, 1885.
M: Ralph Kinzie.
(No children)

265. Lydia White.
B: October 14, 1887.
M: Claude Humbert.
(Had 5 children)

266. John White.
B: November 20, 1889.
M: Amy Traut.
(Had 2 children)

267. Laura White.
B: February 26, 1892.
M: Frank Butterbaugh.
(No children)

268. Hassie White.
B: July 8, 1894.
M: Ben Brantner.
(Had 10 children)

269. Mabel White.
B: April 15, 1897.
M: Casper Sherfy.
(Had 1 child)

270. Pauline White.
B: July 20, 1900.
(Unmarried)

133.
EMANUEL A. BOWMAN
B: October 1, 1857.
M: Mary Harrington,
(They had 2 children.)
They were as follows:

271. William Bowman,
B:
Twice married had 1 son.

272. Joseph Bowman.
B:
(Unmarried)

134.   SAMUEL JOSEPH BOWMAN.
       B: January 18, 1861.
       D: March 4, 1932.
       He was a dentist.
       M: Sue Virginia Bowman(who was a daughter
          of George C. Bowman #120) on August 26, 1886.
       B: May 16, 1863.
       D: March 28, 1906.

       Their children follow:

   273:   Paul Haynes Bowman.
          B: July 5, 1887.
          D:
          M: Flora Hoover on August 12, 1913.
          (They had 4 children.)

   274.   Anna A. Bowman.
          B: October 24, 1888.
          D: May 2, 1954.
          M: Norman A. Seese, on June 6, 1917.
             (They had 5 children)

   275.   J. Price Bowman.
          B: July 5, 1890.
          M: Florence Huff on June 5, 1918.
             (They had 2 children)

   276.   Hazel G. Bowman.
          B: February 22, 1892.
          M: William Cline, on May 4, 1924.
          They had five children.

   277.   G. Nile Bowman.
          B: November 7, 1893.
          D:
          M: Bessie Hodges, on August 30, 1916.
          (They had 4 children.)

   278.   H. C. Early Bowman.
          B: September 12, 1896.
          M: Hattie Cox on October 8, 1933.
                (No children)

   279.   Meriam Bowman.
          B: October 9, 1898.
             (Unmarried)

134.
(Continued:)

Samuel Joseph Bowman's.
(Second Marriage)
M: Virgie Morrell on February 24,1909.
B: December 18,1884.

Their four children are:

280. Ruth Bowman.
B: December 14,1909.
M: James Oppie Bacon on June 29,1935.
(No children)

281. Sue Elizabeth Bowman.
B: December 14,1911.
M: Omer Rowe on September 22,1932.

282. Helen T. Bowman.
B: August 18,1914.
M: Frank Isenberg on May 15,1937.

283. Sarah Janice Bowman.
B: April 18,1926.
M: Clarence Denny. on August 24,1946.

135. Mary S. BOWMAN.
B: July 7,1864.
M: Richard Harrington.

These were their children:
284. Pearl Harrington.

285. Frank Harrington.

286. Harry Harrington.

287. Susan Harrington.

288. Kathleen Harrington.

136. JOHN P. BOWMAN.
B: July 4,1871.
M: Tennie Garst.

These were their children:
289. Ola Bowman.

290. Rowland Bowman. (Died in Infancy).

291. Earl Bowman. (Prominent member of Church of the Brethren.
292. Mary Sue Bowman.
293. Ralph Bowman.
294. Mabel Bowman.
295. Cathaleen Bowman.

JOHN ED BOWMAN.
B: October 1, 1839.
His wife was named Betty.

John Ed in 1914 was living in Wirtz, Virginia on the old home place. Was at this time 75 years of age, was paraly-zed February 1,1912,and was helpless. His wife "Bettie" is a year his senior and in good health at that time. They have had twelve children, six girls, and six boys, three of whom died in infancy.

Two are living in Virginia, five in Ohio, one in Indiana and one in California in 1914, all married and doing well. The following letter was received from him in 1906 and written to Thomas Anderson Bowman #113 page 12 a cousin of John Ed's.

Wirtz, Va. R.F.D. #1
January 19, 1906.

Dear Cousin:

After some indolence and a spell of grip, from which I am just recovering, I will answer your surprised but most welcome letter, received some time ago.

Yes, I am a son of Joel J. Bowman, who was a son of your Uncle John, and Aunt Porizade Bowman. I was born in the house your father Benjamin lived in when he ran your Uncle John Bowman's mill. The old mill is all gone, but a fine roller mill stands just below. The dwelling house is still all right and nice yet. I have your fathers old wooden clock yet, a good one, too. I sold grand-father's a few days ago for $25.00-a good old wooden clock-as a relic. I was the executor of the will of my father, who left the mill to take care of Grandfather, and died soon after in his 41st year. Grandfather chose me to take care of him and Grandmother. She died sudden-ly in her 79th year and Grandfather in his 89th, both dieing at once. He was strong and well until two years before his death. A good man I think he was.

Myself, Daniel A. Bowman of Calico Rock, Va; and David L. Bowman of Devil's Lake, North Dakota, are all the grand children he has of Bowman name. Uncle Lee H. Bowman went to Illinois before I can recollect; Uncle Jack, if living, is in Boone County, West Virginia. Our Uncle Daniel Bowman was a deacon in the Dunkard church, and a nice man. He has been dead quite a while, but has a large number of descendants in this county, and Uncle Chris's people are in Floyd County--a lot of them there are, too but I do not know their post office addresses.

I have never known one of the name with a bad reput-ation and that is something for us to think of and even to boast of, if we wished, but we will let someone else do that if they wish. But the Bowman name stands high so far as I have ever heard, and that is a consolation to us.

Well a little family history. Myself and wife have raised twelve (12) children. We have 53 grand-children. Our baby boy just married Christmas in Ohio and is here on a visit with his wife now. Of our children, some are in Virginia, some in Ohio, some in Indiana, and some in California.

137 - John Edd Bowman (Continued

That's the way we scatter. Myself and wife and all of our children and many grand-children belong to the old Dunkard, or German Baptist church, except our oldest son who went off into politics. He is a Commissioner of Revenue under appointment of the government, and is a strong Republican. No other Bowman I know of is in politics. Most of them are church members and a good many preachers. I am 66 years old in October. My Grandmother was a daughter of John Ferguson, and my mother was a daughter of John Layman. She is 86 years old and very peart yet. Has married the third time and her two last husbands were Dunkard preachers. One of my sons and two sons-in-law are preachers and one a deacon.

Brother David L. Bowman #140 of North Dakota is a preacher. Uncle Daniel Bowman's only son living is named Daniel and is a good Dunkard preacher. Uncle Daniel's children, grand-children and great-grandchildren mostly live in the west end of Franklin County, while we live in the middle or east end of the county.

I do not know what more to write, and if you want to know any more please write again. I should like to have the address of your brother, Benjamin Lee. He ran away from you all in our younger days and came to see us, but went back. When I was in Missouri I thought to go to see him, but found another B.L. Bowman in Newton County, Missouri.

From your well wishing Cousin,

John E. Bowman.

Being unable to secure the record of John and Betty Bowman's children, the historian leaves a number for each that maybe some day some one can supply the names of each of the children;

296. _____ B: D:

297. _____ B: D:

298. _____ B: D:

299. _____ B: D:

300. _____ B: D:

301. _____ B: D:

302. _____ B: D:

303. _____ B: D:

304. _____ B: D:

305. _____ B: D:

306. _____ B: D:

307. _____ B: D:

146. **GEORGE BOWMAN,**
B: November 20, 1847,
D: July 4, 1919.
M: Emily Mildred Akers on February 10, 1870, she was born January 26, 1851, and was the daughter of Nathaniel S, and Elizabeth (Boone) Akers of Franklin County, Virginia.
(The only record we have is as follows:

309. Mary Elizabeth Bowman.
B: October 22, 1875.
M: Thomas Hardin Bowman #164, on Feb 20, 1896.
B: March 2, 1864.

164. **THOMAS HARDIN BOWMAN.**
B: March 2, 1864.
M: Mary Elizabeth Bowman, daughter of George Bowman #146.

The children of Mary Elizabeth & Thomas Hardin Bowman are as follows:

310. Ester May Bowman,
B: May 9, 1897.
M: Terry W, Peters
Resided in Roanoke, Va.

311. Florence Emily Bowman,
B: September 18, 1898.
M: Earl R. White,
Resided in Roanoke, Va.

312. George Erwin Bowman.
B: April 19, 1900.
D: September 29, 1900.

313. Emmert Owens Bowman.
B: July 11, 1901.
M: Elizabeth Wargo.
He was Manager J.J. Newberry Co Stores, Inc in Malone, New York.

314. Fred Edward Bowman.
B: August 4, 1903.
M: Lillian Layman, Resided in Roanoke, Va.

315. Ruth Ann Bowman,
B: December 35, 1904.
M: Glenwood H. Lucas, Resided in Roanoke, Va.

316. Charles Abraham Bowman,
B: November 11, 1907.
M: Nora Evans, Resided in Roanoke, Va.

317. Eva Catherine Bowman.
B: October 23, 1910
M: Warren Creasy,

164. (Continued.

318. Carl Thomas Bowman,
B: August 28, 1913.
M: Louise Bradly,

319. Joel Christ Bowman.
B: June 10, 1916.
M: Helen Strickler, who resides in Roanoke, Va.

216. AMY SOPHIA BOWMAN.
B: September 23, 1857.
D: May 18, 1899.
M: Robert Baldridge,
B: February 4, 1834.
D: December 11, 1895.
Amy and Robert Baldridge had the following children:

320. Herbert Baldridge,
B: July 28, 1879.
D: December 5, 1947.
M: Mary Ellen Storm,
B: March 30, 1882.
D:

321. Irene Baldridge.
B: August 26, 1881.
D: August 20, 1943.
M: Samuel Folsom Fortis,
B: November 2, 1873.
D: August 18, 1929.

322. Robert Lee Baldridge.
B: June 30, 1889.
D:
M: Alice Elizabeth Lalumendier, Jan 24,
B: April 30, 1885.   1910.
D:

217. WILLIAM CHESLEY BOWMAN.
(For his Biography see page 115-A)
B: September 27, 1859
D: April 22, 1950.
M: Emma Estes,
B: February 1, 1864.
D: January 5, 1938.

William and Emma Bowman had ten (10) children, and are as follows:

323. Lyman Russell Bowman, Sr.
B: October 12, 1883.
D:
M: Hita Claudia Gilbreath
B: July 1, 1887.
D: July 15, 1954.

217 (Continued on #32.)   (they had 3 children)

217 Continued.

32.

324. Eula Clippard Bowman.
B: November 11, 1885.
D:
M: William Thomas Shanks.
B: March 22, 1880.
D: August 29, 1926.
(They had 1 child)

325. Joseph Bowman.
B: January 3, 1899.
D:
M: Margaret E. Vaughan
B: September 26, 1888.
D:
(They had 2 daughters.)

326. Lee Reed Bowman.
B: January 25, 1891.
D:
M: Verna Ester Cox.
B: March 21, 1897.
D:

327 Samuel Schuyler Bowman.
B: May 13, 1893.
D:
M: Illa Fowler.
B: October 7, 1894.
D:
(They had 3 children).

328. Arnold Paul Bowman.
B: February 15, 1896.
D: February 7, 1948.
M: Margaret Emily Dover.
B: April 8, 1895.
D:
(They had 3 children.)

329. Robert Byron Bowman.
B: February 27, 1899.
D:
M: Ruby Evans.
B: December 15, 1899.
D:
(They have 2 daughters.)

330. Melvin Emogene Bowman.
B: May 26, 1901.
D:
M: Milam Laban Limbaugh.
B: September 23, 1902.
D:
(No children)

217 Continued.

33.

- 331. Mildred Rebecca Bowman.
  B: December 23, 1903.
  D:
  M: Dr. Lester Paul Hulick, on Aug 18, 1927.
  B: March 26, 1899.
  D: August 20, 1944.
  (They have 2 sons.)

- 332. William Chesley Bowman, Jr.
  B: July 21, 1907
  D:
  M: Ellen Sanderson
  B: December 30, 1907.
  D:
  (They have 2 sons at this writing.)

218. CHARLES CHRISTOPHER BOWMAN.
(For his Biography see page #139.)
B: September 4, 1861.
D: February 4, 1906.
M: Martha Emeline Whitener (Bedford)
B: February 14, 1853.
D: October 14, 1935.
They had five children, and were as follows:

- 333. Curtis Burette Bowman.
  B: August 14, 1884.
  D: December 12, 1953.
  M: Dee Dysart.
  B: June 9, 1884.
  D:
  (They had 1 daughter)

- 334. Claud Whitener Bowman.
  B: July 19, 1887.
  D: March 12, 1891. Age 3 yrs 8 mo.

- 335. Byron Whitener Bowman.
  B: July 24, 1890.
  D:
  M: (1) Ruth Bernice Blankenship.
  B: August 5, 1893.
  D: June 14, 1920.
  (two children by this marriage)
  M: (2) Lillie May Shehorn
  B: August 18, 1899.
  D: June 5, 1952.
  (They had 1 son by this marriage.)

218 (Continued) 34.

336. Ruth Lee Bowman.
B: March 18, 1892.
D:
M: (1) Elmer Lee Smythe.
B: September 29, 1891.
D:
M: (2) Franklyn Howlett Bellamy.
B: April 23, 1892.   M: 9/11.25
D: (Divorced)
(There were 2 daughters by the (1) marriage.)
(None by the (2) marriage.)

337. Golden Virginia Bowman.
B: August 16, 1893.
D:
M: (1) James Clarence White. 7/11,
B: March 19, 1892.   1915.
D: October 21, 1918.
M: (2) George Arthur Evans, 8/24/
B: September 6, 1868.   1922.
D: November 2, 1940.
(There were 2 children by this marriage.)

220.
NETTIE BOWMAN.
B: June 19, 1866.
D: February 4, 1948.
M: Thomas Joseph Jordan. 6/29/1891.
B: March 21, 1864.
D: September 1, 1937.
The following children of Joe & Nettie Jordan:

338. Pauline Jordan.
B: September 18, 1892.
D:
(Unmarried)

339. Geraldine Jordan.
B: August 27, 1894.
D:
M: James Holmes Meek. M: 8/18/1917.
B: February 21, 1896.
D: November 29, 1942.
(They have 1 daughter)

340. Maple Ford Jordan.
B: July 31, 1899.
D: January 30, 1900. Age 6 mo.

221.

SAMUEL LEE BOWMAN.
B: September 11, 1868.
D: July 6, 1949.
M: (1) Annie Gherman, on June 22, 1892.
B: March 25, 1871.
D: May 18, 1927.
M: (2) Edna McCloy (Leeper).
B: April 14, 1880.
D: June 15, 1956.
  Three children by first marriage, and
  none by the second.

The children by Samuel Lee and Annie Bowman,
or as follows:

341. Norma Louese Bowman.
B: November 19, 1906.
D:
M: Ted Higgins.
B: February 16, 1906.
D:
  They have one daughter.

1941247

342. Edgar Gherman Bowman.
B: September 6, 1907.
D:
M:
D:

343. Samuel Lee Bowman, Jr.
B: November 4, 1912.
D:
M: Frances W. Walker.
B: February 29, 1916.
D:
  They have 3 children.

222.

JAMES REED BOWMAN.
  (See his Biography on page No. 163-B.)
B: October 21, 1870
D:
M: Lillie B. Lively.
B: September 17, 1873.
D:
They have the following children:

344. Hinkle Jordan Bowman.
B: February 13, 1894.
D:
M: Lillian Alma Pape.
D:
  (They have one (1) daughter.)

345. Richard Earl Bowman.
B: May 18, 1896.
D:
M: Myrtle Cramer. (They have 3 children)
B: February 16, 1896.
D:

222. (Continued)
James Reed Bowman.

36.

346. Anice Lilyan Bowman.
B: October 6,1900.
D:
M: Ray S.Duncan.
B: October 16,1905.
D:
(They have 1 son.)

347. Myrtle Marguerite Bowman.
B: October 31,1903.
D:
M: Robert Bryce Goodwin.
B: January 10,1902.
D:
(Have 3 children)

223. THOMAS FORD BOWMAN.
B: November 6, 1872.
D: December 27,1935.
M: Minnie Marie Van Doren.
B: September 27, 1872.
D: April 2, 1953.
Their children are as follows:

348. Charlie Wells Bowman.
B: June 3, 1901.
D:
M: Fern Marie Scott.
B: September 30,1900.
D:
"It is said that Charlie had three (3) other marriages, but unable to obtain definite records relative to them."

349. Milton Paul Bowman.
B: February 26,1903.
D:
M: Velma Mary Chilton.
B: July 5, 1911.
(No Children)

225. JOSEPH MAPLE BOWMAN.
B: June 12, 1877.
D: January 31,1952.
M: (1) Lillie Donaldson,on Sep't 15,1901
B: April 6, 1883.
D: December ,1904.
(No children by this marriage.)

M: (2) Minnie I. Brodnax,
B: June 15, 1882.
D: November 13, 1955.
(Four (4) Children by this marriage

350. Lillie B. Bowman.
B: March 20,1906.
D:
M: Lewis C.Yates. (No children.)
B: May 30,1906.
D:

225. (Continued)
Joseph Maple. Bowman.

351. Benjamin Lee Bowman.
B: June 30, 1907.
D:
M: Bernice Irene Baile,
B: March 22, 1911.
D:
(They have 2 children.)

352. Em Harlan Bowman.
B: December 8, 1909.
D:
M: (1) Mary Louise Jones, (Divorced.
B: In 1908.
(1 child by this marriage.)
D:
M: (2) Neva Catherine Cox.
B: May 14, 1921.
D:
(1 child by this marriage)

353. Adelaide Bowman.
B: June 20, 1919.
D:
M: (1) James Leo Harvey. (Divorced)
B: December 22, 1919.
D:
(Two children by this marriage.)
M: (2) R.P.Lynn,
B: ?
D: ?
(One child by this marriage.)

226. WILBUR TALLEY BOWMAN.
B: December 22, 1878.
D: June 29, 1940.
M: Hattie Donaldson. Sept 15, 1901.
B: June 6, 1881.
D:
(They had 4 children.)

354. James D. Bowman.
B: January 7, 1903.
D:
M: Catherine Anna Dodge,
B: August 16, 1903.
D:
(They have 2 children.)

355. Lillie B. Bowman.
B: June 14, 1904.
D:
M: Thomas Lawrence Hallahan.
B: July 16, 1905.
D:
(Have 1 child.)

356. Wilbur J. Bowman.
B: June 16, 1906.
D:
M: Mary Catherine Cubbins. Oct 12,
B: August 28, 1906.   1936.
D:

226.(Continued).
Wilbur T.Bowman.

38,

357. Woodrow W.Bowman.
B: March 12, 1914.
D:
M: Billie Harrison.
B: October 11, 1915.
D:
(They have 1 daughter.)

227. ANNA BOWMAN.
B: October 20,1880.
D: August 1,1955.
M: Thomas Alexander Abernathy.
B: November 11, 1870.
D: April 6, 1938.
(They have 7 children.)

358. Louella Abernathy.
B: May 4, 1901.
D:
(1) M:(1) John D.McNabb,Sr.
B: ?
D: Divorced 6/10/
(2) M: Charles Henry Banes.   1923.
on June 11,1924.
B: December 20,1893.
D: September 19,1952.
(Had 1 child by first marriage,
none by the second).

359. Sara Lee Abernathy.
B: February 7,1905.
D: May 9,1941.
M: Joseph Noser.
B: October 11,1900.
D: March 8, 1937.
(They had one daughter.)

360. Geraldine Abernathy.
B: November 2,1906.
D:
M: Fred Jackson.
B: December 24,1895.
D:
(Have no Children.)

361. Anna Abernathy.
B: January 28, 1912.
D:
M: David Hunter.
B: October 12,1910.
D:
(They have 2 Children)

362. Melvin Abernathy.
B: June 28, 1914.
D:
M: Samuel Massey.
B: January 28, 1916.
D:
(They have 2 Children.)

227 (Continued)
Anna Abernathy.

363. Thomas Alexander Abernathy, Jr.
B: August 10, 1916.
D:
M: Edythe Whitehead.
B: August 8, 1918.
D:
(They have 2 Children.)

364. Nettie Jane Abernathy.
B: March 24, 1921.
D:
M: John H. Hackney.
B: March 10, 1922.
(They have three children at this writing.)
D:

241. BENJAMIN LEE WELKER.
B: November 28, 1869.
D:
M: Ellen Owens, (Called Nell)
B: September 14, 1867.
D: May   , 1914.
(They had three children.) follows:

365. Eugenia Welker.
B: September 6, 1892.
D:
(Unmarried)

366. Guadeta I. Welker.
B: August 9, 1894 at Marquand, Mo.
D: November 18, 1918 at Milford, Utah, with the Influenza, while teaching there in the Public Schools.
(Unmarried).

367. Benjamin Lee Welker, Jr.
B: August 4, 1896. Teaching in a College, Stokton, Cal.
D:
M:
B:
D:

244. JAMES F. WELKER.
B: November 8, 1883.
D:
M: Herscella Anna Pair.
B: November 15, 1886.
D: June 12, 1941.
(Their children were):

368. Clara P. Welker.
B: March 29, 1912.
D:
M: Albert Warner.
B:
D:

244 (Continued)
James F. Welker.

369. Woodrow William Welker.
B: June 10, 1914.
D:
M: Mary Frances Stover, Sep't 2, 1939.
D:

370. Mary Irene Welker.
B: September 27, 1916.
D:
M: (1) Edward Bennett,
(1 child by this marriage.)
B:
D:
M: (2) Elmer Taylor.
(No children by this marriage.)

245.

JOHN J. BOWMAN. (See Biography page #41)
B: August 30, 1874.
D:
M: Betty Hill, on October 4, 1905.
B: June 16, 1876.
D: September 28, 1953.
They had one daughter as follows:

371. Georgia Bessie Bowman.
B: May 20, 1914.
D:

248.

BESSIE BEULAH BOWMAN.
B: July 20, 1882.
D: July 27, 1912, at Williamsville, MO.
M: John Willis Alexander, on 6/12/05.
B:
D:
(No children)

249.

THOMAS DEWITT BOWMAN. (See Biography on
B: March 14, 1886.   Page # 43.
D:
M: Lillian Parker.
B: August 16, 1886, Freeport, Nova
D: Scotia, Canada.
These are their children:

372. Thomas Parker Bowman.
B: June 19, 1917.
D:
M: Sheila Goodall Fraser.
B: August 6, 1921.
D:

373. Patricia Hamilton Bowman.
B: April 24, 1920.
D:
M: Dr. Amos Johnson Shaler. (D. SC.)
B: July 8, 1917, in London, England, of
American parentage. Head of the
Department of Metallurgy-Penn
State University.
D:

JOHN J. BOWMAN
(Biography)

John Jasper Bowman, oldest son of T.A. and Emma Bowman, was born at Pocahontas, Cape Girardeau County Missouri., August 30, 1874. He was educated in the public schools of Jackson, Salem, Pacific, and Steelville, Missouri., and graduated from the high School at Slater, Mo1891, being the first boy to graduate from that High School. He spent four years in William Jewell College, at Liberty, Mo., graduating with the degree of A.B. in 1897. His college course was interrupted by one year of work to obtain funds with which to finish his education. He taught in Will Mayfield College, Marble Hill, Mo., and was employed in the office of the Dunklin Democrat, at Kennett, Mo., in 1895. While in College he was awarded gold medals in essay and oratorical contests and represented William Jewell College twice in the State Inter-Collegiate contests, at Sedalia in 1894, and at Kansas City in 1896. In speaking to him by his father, Dr. J.P. Greene, president of the College, once said: "We never had, and we never will have a better student in College!" That statement was always a source of great joy and satisfaction to the father.

John had no easy time in College, for funds were scarce and he spent much time working in the newspaper offices in Liberty, being a good printer, and thus paid most of his expenses. This work was not allowed to interfere with his studies, however, for he always kept up with all of his classes and took part in all the activities of college life. He took a prominent part in literary society work and in his senior year was elected June President of the Excelsior Society, one of the honors of college life. He was a charter member of Alpha-Omega chapter of the Kappa Sigma fraternity.

After his graduation from William Jewell College he taught in Farmington, Mo., a short time and then engaged in newspaper work at Salem, Maryville, Lathrop, Liberty, and Louisiana, Mo., editing papers at Salem, and Louisiana. In 1901 he engaged in the banking business, going to Lake City, Arkansas., where he opened the Farmers and Merchants Bank and was Cashier for more than two years. His health having become impaired by malaria, he returned to Missouri in 1905, after having been connected for a short time temporarily with the State National Bank of Little Rock, Ark., and went to Bonne Terre, Mo., as Cashier of the Bank of Bonne Terre, which had just been established.

In 1907 he accepted a position with the Farmers & Miners Trust Co, at Bonne Terre, one of the largest banks in the smaller towns of the State at that time, and remained until 1913, when it liquidated its business. He then organized the Peoples Bank of Bonne Terre, and was Cashier and later President. When the Federal Deposit Insurance Corporation was established in 1932 he was appointed as one of the first examiners in Missouri and served in the western part of the state until his retirement. Later he entered business again and was connected with the Libert Marketing Company several years, and was Manager of a wholesale brokerage house in Kansas City, Missouri., for some time. In 1954 he was appointed City Treasurer of Liberty, Missouri., to fill a vacancy caused by the death of the former Treasurer.

He was married in St. Louis, Mo; October 4, 1905, to Miss Betty Hill, daughter of George W. and Helen Turner Hill, formerly of St. Clair County, Illinois. She was educated in the public schools of St Louis and graduated from Washington University in St Louis with the degree of A.B., magna cum laude, in 1897. She then taught language in Liberty Ladies College at Liberty, Mo., for six years, until her marriage. (See next page.)

Biography
John J. Bowman. (Continued)

She was outstanding as a linguist, being noted for her knowledge of German, French, Spanish, Latin and Greek, all of which she taught at various times. After the family moved to Liberty, Missouri she taught language in William Jewell College for ten years.
She died in Liberty, Mo, September 28, 1953, after an illness of two and one-half years.
One daughter, Georgia Bessie, was born of this union, at Bonne Terre, Missouri., May 20, 1914. After graduating from the public High school at Bonne Terre, she was graduated from William Jewell College at Liberty in 1934. She attended the school of Journalism of the University of Missouri at Columbia and receiving the degree of Bachelor of Journalism there. She received the degree of Master of Arts in speech and radio at the State University of Iowa, Iowa City, Iowa. She taught in the high schools of Liberty and Hannibal, Missouri., and after graduating from Iowa State University was connected with radio station WLW at Cincinnati. She next taught radio news broadcasting in the School of Journalism at the University of Missouri in Columbia and during World War II took a leave of absence and was Director of Radiobroadcasting for the American Red Cross in the 17 states of the Midwestern area. She taught in the speech Department of Brooklyn College, Brooklyn, N.Y., one year and then returned to Liberty as Director of forensics, debate coach and teacher of Journalism in William Jewell College, where she now is.
JOHN J, is a Baptist and a Freemason, being a Past Master of Samaritan Lodge No. 424, A.F. & A.M., Bonne Terre, Mo., Past High Priest of Uel Chapter No. 129, Bonne Terre, and of Liberty Chapter No. 3, Royal Arch Masons, Liberty, Mo., Past Illustrious Master of Bonne Terre Council No. 43, Royal and Select Masters, Bonne Terre, Mo., Past Eminent Commander of DeSoto Commandery No. 56, Knights Templar, DeSoto, Mo., and of Liberty Commandery No. 6, K.T., Liberty, Mo., former District Deputy Grand Master of the 48th Masonic District of Missouri for eight years and District Deputy Grand Master of the 11th Masonic District of Missouri for five years; a member of the Missouri Lodge of Research, the Order of High Priesthood, Order of the Silver Trowel, Past Commanders Association of Knights Templar of Missouri and Knight of the York Court of Honor.

This record goes to show that a BOWMAN can be successful without being a preacher, a miller, or raising a BIG family.

Hats off to you John old boy!!!!!!!!!!!!!!!!!!!!!!!!!!!!!!!
                                      Byron W. Bowman, Historian.

BIOGRAPHY OF
THOMAS DEWITT BOWMAN

Thomas DeWitt Bowman, the youngest living child of T.A. and Emma Bowman, was born in Pacific, Missouri Franklin County, on March 14, 1886.

He went through the public schools of Jackson, and Fredericktown, Missouri, and graduated from the Fredericktown High School in 1901.

While attending high school he belonged to the high school cadets, a military department of the high school. He then attended Marvin Collegiate Institute, a Methodist school at Fredericktown, for two years. During this time he spent his vacation in his father's printing office, and became a printer.

In 1907 he received his A.B. degree from William Jewell College, completing the required course in a little over three years.

After his graduation from college he worked at various occupations finally going back to his old printing trade at Bloomfield, Missouri, where he remained until 1909, when he went to Corder, Mo and established The Corder Journal. Later he sold this newspaper, and bought the Democrat-Herald at Smithville, Missouri.

In 1911 he received an appointment in the American Consular service, and afterselling his Smithville paper, he went to Nogales, Sonora Mexico as clerk and later as Vice-Consul and Consul in the American Consular office there.

He served many years in Mexico, with an interval of service at Fernie, British Columbia, during the days of the Caranza Revolution, when all Americans had to leave Mexico, but returned there later for service at a number of points in Mexico.

During his years of service he was advanced until he reached the highest grade as Consul General, and in this time was stationed at Budapest, Hungary; Santiago, Chile; Belfast, Ireland; Naples, Italy; Johannesburg, Union South Africa; Canton, China; which was his last post.

He retired after more than thirty six (36) years in the service of the State Department, and has since made his home at 32 Wall Street, Wellesley, Massachusetts.

He was married to Miss Lillian Parker, a native of Novia Scotia, Canada, whom he met in Fernie, British Columbia, while serving there, and she teaching in the schools there.

They have two children, Thomas Parker, who is married and have three (3) small sons, he is in the Public Relations Department of the Ralph M. Parsons Construction Co, of New York, N.Y. He graduated from the Massachusetts Institute of Technology at Boston, Mass. He attended school abroad; Woodberry Forrest in Virginia. He served in the Army as a Meteroligist and during World War II, retiring as MAJOR.

Patricia (Pat) attended schools abroad; Penn Hall at Chambersburg, Penn, and Pine Manor Junior College at Wellesley, Mass. She married Dr. Amos Johnson Shaler, D.SC, head of the department of Metalurgy at Pennsylvania State University, at State College, Penn. They have two daughters, and one son at this writing.

250. ORREN CLYDE BOWMAN.
B: December 6, 1887.
D: February 17, 1888.

256. J. ROBERT BOWMAN.
B: November 20, 1869.
D: January 25, 1909.
M: Julia Keefaver.
B:
D:
(Said to have had 4 children, one of which is:
374. J.R. Bowman, of Johnson City, Tennessee, a prominent child specialist.

259. WALTER H. BOWMAN.
B: February 8, 1878.
D: August 1949, Age 77 years.
M:
B:
D:
(Said to have had 1 daughter names Lola)

260. RUEL BOWMAN PRITCHETT.
B:
D:
M:
B:
D:
(A minister in church of the Brethren and lives at White Pine, Tennessee.)

273. PAUL HAYNES BOWMAN.
B: July 5, 1887.
D:
M: Flora Hoover.
B: August 12, 1913.
D:
The children of Dr. Paul & Flora Bowman were as follows:

375. Paul Hoover Bowman.
B: June 20, 1914.
D:
M: Evelyn Stauffer.
B:
D:

376. Grace Bowman.
B: October 8, 1917.
D:
M: Robert Koons, on Jan 1, 1949.
B: July 11, 1917.
D:

377. John Evans Bowman.
B: April 23, 1920.
D:
M: Virginia Kerlin, on July 10, 1945.
B: September 4, 1920.
D:

273. Continued.

274.

275.

378. Rebecca Gene Bowman.
B: January 1, 1925.
D:
M: Charley B. Johnson, on March 21, 1953.
B: June 1, 1924.
D:

ANNA A. BOWMAN.
B: October 24, 1888.
D: May 2, 1954.
M: Norman A. Seese, on June 6, 1917.
B:
D:

379. Norman A. Seese, Jr.
B:
D:
M: Ruth Rice,
B:
D:

380. Margaret Bowman.
B:
D:
M: De Neal Dean.
B:
D:

381. Sylvia Bowman.
B:
D:
M: (Unmarried)

382. Lyman Bowman.
B:
D:
M: Rose Mary Texiere,
B:
D:

383. Patricia Bowman.
B:
D:
M: Joseph Heiney,
B:
D:

J. PRICE BOWMAN,
B:
D:
M:
B:
D:

384. Louise Bowman.
B:
D:
M: George Nipe.
B:
D:

275.
(Continued)

276.

    385. Rosa Lee Bowman.
        B:
        D:
        M. Hugh Moomaw. (They had 1 child)
        B:
        D:
   Hazel G. Bowman.
      B: February 22, 1892.
      D:
      M: William Cline.
      B:
      D:
      Their Children:
    386. Doris Cline.
        B:
        D:
        M: Robert Richards, a preacher and a Champion Pole Vaulter "Olympics 2nd place as World Champion.
    387. Mary Cline.
        B:
        D:
        M: Paul St Claire.
        B:
    388. Joan Cline.
        B:
        D:
        M: Robert Jenkins.
        B:
    390. Samuel Cline.
        B:
        D: (Unmarried)

277.
   G. Nile Bowman.
      B: November 7, 1893.
      D:
      M: Bessie Hodges, on Aug 30, 1916.
      B:
      D:
      Their Children as follows:
    391. Dorothy Bowman.
        B:
        D:
        M: Marvin Howard.
        B:
        D:
    392. Christine Bowman.
        B:
        D:
        M: Eddie Thornton.
        B:
    393. Stanley Bowman.
        B:
        D:
        (Unmarried)

47.
394. **G. Nile Bowman, Jr.**
    B:
    D:
    (Unmarried)

281. SUE ELIZABETH BOWMAN.
    B: December 14, 1911.
    D:
    M: Omer Rowe, on Sep't 22, 1932.
    B:
    D:
        Their Children as follows:
395. Susanne Rowe.
    B:
    D:
    M
    B:
    D:
396. Evelyn Rowe.
    B:
    D:
    M:
    B:
    D:

282. Helen T. Bowman.
    B: August 18, 1926.
    D:
    M: Frank Isenberg, on Sep't 22, 1932.
    B:
    D:
        Their children=
397. John E. Bowman
    B:
    D:
    M:
    B:
    D:
398. Lucy Ellen Bowman.
    B:
    D:
    M:
    B:
    D:
399. Ann Bowman.
    B:
    D:
    M:
    B:
    D:

283. Sarah Janice Bowman.
    B: April 18, 1926.
    D:
    M: Clarence Dennyson, on Aug 24, 1946.
    B:
    D:
        Their Children:=
400. _____
    B:
    D:

48.

310. ESTER MAY BOWMAN.
B: May 9, 1897.
D:
M: Terry W. Peters. Resided in Roa-
B: noke, Virginia.
D:
Their Children are:
401. Hazel Marie Peters.
B: April 2, 1919.
D:
M:
402. Geraldine Peters.
B: June 17, 1922.
D:
M:

311. Florence Emily Bowman.
B: September 18, 1898.
D:
M: Earl Ray White.
B:
D:
Their Children=
403. Thelma Ruth White.
B: April 15, 1919.
D:
M:
B:
404. Dorothy Aileene White.
B: May 11, 1921.
D:
M:
B:

313. EMMERT OWENS BOWMAN.
B: July 11, 1901. Was Mgr J.J. Newberry
D: Co store in Malone,
M: Elizabeth Wa- N.Y.
rgo.
B:
(They had one child) =
405. Virginia Elaine Bowman.
B: May 14, 1939.
D:
M:

314. FRED EDWARD BOWMAN
B: August 4, 1903. (Resided in Roan-
D: oke, Va.
M: Lillian Layman.
B:
D:
Their Children are:
406. Robert Bowman.
B: March 28, 1931.
D:
M:
407: Betty Ann Bowman.
B: May 13, 1935.
D:
M:

49.

315.
RUTH ANN BOWMAN. Resided in Roanoke, Va.
- B: December 25, 1904.
- D:
- M: Glenwood H. Lucas,
- B:
- D:

408. Marlene Lucas.
- B: September 27, 1932.
- D:
- M:

316.
CHARLES ABRAHAM BOWMAN.
- B: November 11, 1907.
- D:
- M: Nora Evans.
- They had 2 children and have no records on them.

409. _____
- B:
- D:
- M:

410. _____
- B:
- D:
- M:

317.
EVA CATHERINE BOWMAN.
- B: October 23, 1910. Resided Roanoke, Va.
- D:
- M: Warren Creasy.
- B:
- D:
- They had 2 children, no records.

411. _____
- B:
- D:
- M:

412. _____
- B:
- D:
- M:

318.
CARL THOMAS BOWMAN
- B: August 28, 1913.
- D:
- M: Louise Bradley.
- Had 2 Children, no records.

413. _____
- B:
- D:
- M:

414. _____
- B:
- D:
- M:

319:
JOEL CHRIST BOWMAN.
- B: June 10, 1916.
- D:
- M: Helen Strickler. (Had 1 Child.)

415. Martha Ellen Bowman.
- B:

50.

320.
HERBERT BALDRIDGE.
B: July 28, 1879.
D: December 5, 1947.
M: Mary Ellen Storm.
B: March 30, 1882.

Their children are as follows:
416. William Herbert, Baldridge.
B: August 31, 1909.
D:
M: Margaret H. Carrell.
B: June 28, 1917.
D:
417. John Harold, Baldridge.
B: February 19, 1913.
D: July 12, 1943.
M: Estella Mills in 1934.
He was killed by the enemy fire at Gaudacanal, Henderson Flying Field. Was a C.P.O. and deep sea Diver.

321.
IRENE BALDRIDGE.
B: August 26, 1881.
D: August 20, 1943.
M: Samuel Folsom Portis.
B: November 2, 1873.
D: August 18, 1929.
(Their children were:)
418. Jewell D. Portis,
B: April 26, 1902.
D:
M: Emmett L. Heady.
B: September 28, 1900.
D:
(Had 2 Children)
419. Bessie Elizabeth Portis.
B: May 2, 1907.
D:
M: Roy Fox.
B: September 4, 1892.
D:

322.
ROBERT LEE BALDRIDGE.
B: June 30, 1889.
D:
M: Alice Elizabeth Lalumendier.
B: April 30, 1885.
D:
Their children were:
420. Amy Elizabeth Baldridge.
B: October 20, 1911.
D:
M: Clifford W. Wilson, on Aug 19, 1941.
D:
421. William Joseph Baldridge.
B: August 7, 1920.
D:
M: Geraldine Stoff.
B: February 22, 1922.
D:

323. LYMAN RUSSELL BOWMAN.
    B: October 12,1883.
    D:
    M: Hita Claudia Gilbreath.
    B. July 1,1887.
    D. July 15,1954.
    Lyman and Hita's children are:

422. Lyman Russell Bowman, Jr.
    B: June 23,1907.
    D:
    M: Lida Bell Powell.
    B: September 17,1907.
    D:
423. Kathleen Ford Bowman.
    B: April 23,1909.
    D:
    M: Bernice Anderson Farmer.
    B: April 18,1920.
424. Benjamin Lee Bowman.
    B: October 18,1920.
    D:
    M. Rita Laurie Heisserer.
    B: April 15,1920.
    D:

324. EULA CLIPPARD BOWMAN.
    B: November 11,1885.
    D:
    M: William Thomas Shanks.
    B: March 22,1880.
    D: August 29,1926.
    Their child was:

425. William Thomas Shanks, Jr.
    B: November 25,1912.
    D: May 24,1914.

325. JOSEPH BOWMAN.
    B: January 3, 1889.
    D:
    M: Margaret E. Vaughn.
    B: September 26,1888.
    D:
    Their children were:
426. Elizabeth V. Bowman.
    B: March 7,1915.
    D:
    M: Narcissee Edward Fuch.
    B: August 7,1910.
    D:
427. Adagene Bowman.
    B: May 20,1917.
    D:
    M: Guy Edwin Dixon, Jr.
    B: August 21,1920.
    D:

326. LEE REED BOWMAN.
B: January 25, 1891.
D:
M: Verna Ester Cox.
B: March 21, 1897.
D:
Lee and Verna's children were:

428. John Webster Bowman.
B: August 9, 1919.
D:
M: Eleanor Noyes Hempstone.
B: September 3, 1924.
D:

429. Lee Austin Bowman.
B: June 30, 1923.
D:
M: Cathleen Carpenter.
B: June 20, 1927.
D:

327. SAMUEL SCHUYLER BOWMAN.
B: May 13, 1893.
D:
M: Illa Fowler.
B: October 7, 1894.
D:
Sam and Illa's children were:

430. Samuel Schuyler Bowman, Jr.
B: February 5, 1915.
D:
M (1) Julia Mattie Fenimore.
B: January 21, 1915.
D: December 21, 1935.
(1 son by this marriage)
M: (2) Josephine Evelyn Hopper.
B: November 23, 1915 in Saskatchewan, Canada, at Abbey.
D:
(Two sons by this marriage.)

431. Eugene Fowler Bowman.
B: August 3, 1917.
D:
M: (1) Rosemary Tallent.
B: May 6, 1917.
D:
(Two children by this marriage)
M: (2) Dorothy Mae Henthorn.
B: July 27, 1924.
D:
(2 Children by this marriage.)

432. Frances Emogene Bowman.
B: February 11, 1921.
D: October 10, 1953.
M: William Henry Simmons.
B: July 7, 1923.
D:
(One Daughter by this marriage)

328.
  ARNOLD PAUL BOWMAN.
    B: February 15,1896.
    D: February 7,1948.
    M: Margaret Emily Dover.
    B: April 8,1895.
    D:
    Paul & Margaret's children were:

  433. Margaret Emily Bowman.
    B: August 15,1918.
    D:
    M: Capt. Robert W. Howard.
    B: July 4,1915.
    D:

  434. Arnold Paul Bowman, Jr.
    B: September 6,1920.
    D:
    M: Jean Linville Wilke.
    B: September 22,1920.
    D:

  435. Phillip Dover Bowman.
    B: November 16,1926.
    D: July 18,1948.

329.
  Robert Byron BOWMAN.
    B: February 27,1899.
    D:
    M: Ruby Evans.
    B: December 15,1899.
    D:
    Byron & Ruby's children were:

  436. Jane Evans Bowman.
    B: October 30,1935.
    D:
    M: Howard Edward Thilenius.
    B: December 25,1936.
    D:

  437. Nancy Ann Bowman.
    B: November 27,1938.
    D:
    M:
    B:
    D:

331.
  MILDRED REBECCA BOWMAN.
    B: December 23,1903.
    D:
    M: Dr. Lester Hulic.
    B: March 26,1899.
    D: August 20,1944.
    Lester & Mildred's children were:
  438. Robert Bowman Hulick.
    B: January 18,1929.
    D:
    M:
    B:
     (See next page Continued.)

331.
Continued+

54.
439. Carl Webster Hulick.
B: January 9, 1935.
D:
M:
B:
D:

332. WILLIAM CHESLEY BOWMAN, JR
B: July 21, 1907.
D:
M: Ellen Sanderson.
B: December 30, 1907.
D:
   Bill and Ellen's Children are:

440. William Chesley,3rd
B: January 16, 1934.
D:
M:
B:
D:

441. John Sanderson Bowman.
B: November 22, 1935.
D:
M:
B:
D:

333. CURTIS BURETTE BOWMAN.
B: August 14,1884.
D: December 12,1953.
M: Dee Dysart.
B: June 9,1881.
Burette and Dee Bowman had a daughter:

442. Margaret Dysart Bowman.
B: April 17,1911.
D:
M: Charles J.Griffith,Sr.
B: January 10, 1908.
D:
   (They have two sons)

334. CLAUDIE W.BOWMAN
B: July 19,1887.
D: March 12,1891.

335. BYRON WHITENER BOWMAN.
B: July 24,1890.
D:
M: (1) Ruth Bernice Blankenship.
B: August 5, 1893. M:9/16/1914.
D: June 14,1920.
   (2 children by the above marriage)
M: (2) Lillie May Shehorn.
B: August 18,1899.
D: June 5, 1952.
   (1 child by this marriage:

335.
(Continued)

Children by Byron & Ruth Bowman:
By their first Marriage:

443. Charles Dale Bowman.
B: February 28,1916.
D:
M: Sally Mable Pass.
B: February 19, 1918.
D:
(They have two sons)

444. Ruth Frances Bowman.
B: February 2, 1920.
D:
M: Jay William Miller
B: March 9,1913.
D:
(They have 2 sons)
Child by Byron & Lillie Bowman:
the second marriage:

445. Byron Burette Bowman.
B: November 1,1923.
D:
M: Lethea Ann Davis.
B: February 24,1927.
D:
(At this writing they have 2 daughters.

336.

RUTH LEE BOWMAN.
B: March 18,1892.
D:
M: (1) Elmer Lee Smythe.
B: September 29, 1891.
D: (Divorced.)
There are 2 daughters by this marriage.
M: (2) Franklyn Howlett Bellamy.
B: April 23, 1892.
D:
(No children by this marriage.)

The two daughters by Ruth & Elmer Smythe are:

446. Wilda Virginia Smythe.
B: October 5, 1912.
D:
M: Cloyd Gale Abbott.
B: March 23,1909.
D:
(1 child by this marriage)

447. Mary Lee Smythe.
B: February 7,1915.
D:
M: Frederick Peterson.
B: May 8,1914.
D:
(They have 2 children at this writing.)

56.

337.
GOLDEN VIRGINIA BOWMAN.
B: August 16, 1893.
D:
M: (1) James Clarence White.
B: March 19, 1892.
D: October 21, 1918.
(1 child by this marriage)
M: (2) George Arthur Evans.
B: September 6, 1868.
D: November 2, 1940.
(2 Children by this marriage)
Clarence & Golden White had the following daughter:

448. Virginia Lucille White.
B: September 15, 1918.
D:
M: Ray Willie Rainey.
B: July 6, 1915.
D:

George & Golden Evans had the following children:

449. Charles Arthur Evans.
B: January 27, 1924.
D:
M: Helen LaClede Nichols.
B: October 29, 1928.
D:

450. Georgia Maurine Snider.
B: April 29, 1927.
D:
M: Harold Eugene Snider.
B: July 24, 1925.
D:

339.
GERALDINE JORDAN.
B: August 27, 1894.
D:
M: James Holmes Meek.
B: February 21, 1896.
D: November 29, 1942.
James & Geraldine Meek had the following daughter:

451. Elizabeth Sue (Betsy) Meek.
B: September 4, 1918.
D:
M: George Willard Price.
B: November 20, 1914.
D:
(They have 2 children at this writing)

341.
NORMA LOUESE BOWMAN.
B: November 19, 1906.
D:
M: Ted Higgins.
B: February 16, 1906.
D:
(Continued to page 57.

341.
(Continued)

452. Mary Louese Higgins.
B: January 30, 1926.
D:
M: Warren Litton Smith.
B: November 2, 1922.
D:
(They have 2 Children)

343.
SAMUEL LEE BOWMAN.
B: November 14, 1912.
D:
M: Frances W. Walker.
B: February 29, 1916.
D:
Sam & Frances have 3 children at this writing, and are:

453. Alice Ann Bowman.
B: December 6, 1939.
D:
M:
B:
D:

454. Samuel Lee Bowman, 3rd.
B: October 26, 1942.
D:
M:
B:
D:

455. William Walker Bowman.
B: October 11, 1948.
D:
M:
B:
D:

344.
HINKLE JORDAN BOWMAN.
B: February 13, 1894.
D:
M: Lillian Pape.
B: January 21, 1894.
D:
Hinkle & Lillian Bowman have one daughter:

456. Helen Louise Bowman.
B: January 3, 1916.
D:
M:

345.
RICHARD EARL BOWMAN.
B: May 18, 1896.
D:
M: Myrtle Cramer.
B: February 16, 1896.
D:
Earl & Myrtle Bowman have 3 children as follows:

(Continued page 58.)

345.
(Continued)

58.
457. James Wilson Bowman.
B: November 19,1914.
D:
M: Edna Ruth Davis.
B: July 21,1906.
D:
458. Margaret Bowman.
B: January 26,1916.
D:
M: Hubert Harlice Coates.
B: September 29,1909.
D:
459. Virginia Lee Bowman.
B: August 2,1925.
D:
M: James Henry Timberlake.
B: June 11,1924.
D:

346.
ALICE LILYAN BOWMAN.
B: October 6,1900.
D:
M: Ray S. Duncan.
B: October 16, 1905.
D:
Alice & Ray Duncan have one son:
460. Ray Bowman Duncan.
B: November 19,1935.
D:
M:
B:
D:

347.
MYRTLE MARGUERITE BOWMAN.
B: October 31, 1903.
D:
M: Robert Bryce Goodwin.
B: January 10,1902.
D:
Bob & Marguerite have three sons:
461. Robert Bryce Goodwin, 2nd.
B: May 9,1925.
D:
M: Carol Ann Dunn.
B: July 15,1928.
D:
462. James Lee Goodwin.
B: January 17, 1928.
D:
M: Mary Ernest Clack.
B: September 19, 1927.
D:
463. Lane Alden Goodwin.
B: October 9, 1929.
D:
M: Linda Beebe,
B: November 16,1934.
D:

59.

351.
BENJAMIN LEE BOWMAN, Sr.
    B: June 30, 1907.
    D:
    M: Bernice Irene Haile.
    B: March 22, 1911.
    D:
    Ben & Irene have the following children;
464. Barbara Louise Bowman.
    B: October 7, 1927.
    D:
    M: Jay M. Axtell.
    B: January 9, 1922.
    D:
465. Benjamin Lee Bowman, Jr.
    B: July 30, 1929.
    D:
    M: Sharon Kaye Harwood, June 5, 1955.
    B: June 23, 1937.
    D:

352.
EM HARLAN BOWMAN.
    B: December 8, 1909.
    D:
    M: (1) Mary Louise Jones. (Divorced)
    B: 1908.
    D:
    M: (2) Neva Catherine Cox.
    B: May 14, 1921.
    D:
    (1 daughter by first marriage)
466. Joe Ann Bowman.
    B: March 3, 1931.
    D:
    M: Robert E. Miller.
    B: March 1, 1928.
    D:
    (1 son by second marriage)
467. Joe Thomas Bowman.
    B: June 21, 1944.
    D:
    M:
    B:
    D:

353.
ADELAIDE BOWMAN.
    B: June 20, 1919.
    D:
    M: (1) James Leo Harvey. (Divorced)
    B: December 22, 1919.
    D.
    (2 children by first marriage)
468. Jan Iris Harvey.
    B: July 27, 1940.
    D:
    M:
    B:
    D:
    (Continued on next page # 60)

60.

353.
(Continued)

469. James Michael Harvey.
    B: January 23, 1945.
    D:
    M:
    B:
    D:

    M: (2) R.P. Lynn
    B: ?
    Child by second marriage.

470.* Linda Sue (Lynn).
    * Name of Linda Sue Lynn changed to Linda Sue Harvey by a Court Order.

354.
JAMES DONALDSON BOWMAN.
    B: January 7, 1903.
    D:
    M: Catherine Anna Dodge,
    B: August 16, 1903.
    D:
    James & Catherine's children are:

471. Catherine Anna Bowman.
    B: April 27, 1930.
    D:
    M: Glenn Patrick Seyferth.
    B: October 1929.
    D:

472. Patricia Ann Bowman.
    B: January 13, 1943.
    D:
    M:
    B:
    D:

355.
LILLIE B. BOWMAN.
    B: June 14, 1904.
    D:
    M: Thomas Lawrence Hallahan.
    B: July 16, 1905.
    D:
    Tom & Lillie's Children are:
473. Carole Jean Hallahan.
    B: January 12, 1931.
    D:
    M:
    B:
    D:

356.
WILBUR J. BOWMAN.
    B: June 16, 1906.
    D:
    M: Mary Catherine Gubbins.
    B: August 28, 1906.
    D:

See page 61
(Continued)

356. (Continued)

61.
Wilbur & Mary's children are as follows:
474. Mary Catherine Bowman.
B: November 11, 1937.
D:
M:
B:
D:

475. W. John Joseph Bowman.
B: November 5, 1939.
D:

476. James Joseph Bowman.
B: October 14, 1940
D:
M:

477. Margaret Mary Bowman.
B: June 29, 1942.
D:
M:

478. Robert Joseph Bowman.
B:
D:
M:

357.

WOODROW W. BOWMAN.
B: March 12, 1914.
D:
M: Billie Harrison, on June 1, 1935.
B: October 11, 1915.
D:
Children of Woodrow and Billie are:
479. Joan Elizabeth Bowman.
B: June 25, 1938.
D:
M:
B:
D:

358.

LOUELLA ABERNATHY.
B: May 4, 1901.
D:
M: (1) John D. McNabb, Sr.
B: ?   Divorced on June
D: ?   10, 1923 at St Louis Missouri.
M: (2) Charles Henry Banes, on June
B: Dec 20, 1893.   11, 1924.
L: September 19, 1952.
Child by First Marriage was:
480. John D. McNabb, Jr.
B: November 15, 1920.
D:
M: Irene Nufer.
B: July 23, 1928.
D:

359   SARAH LEE ABERNATHY.
        B: February 7, 1905
        D: May 9, 1941.
        M: Joseph Noser,
        B: October 11, 1900.
        D: March 8, 1937.
        (Their child was.)
    481. Frieda Agnes (Peggy) Noser.
        B: July 24, 1920.
        D:
        M: Audrey H. Nelson, M: Aug 17, 1937.
        B: December 31, 1918.
        D:

361. ANNA ABERNATHY.
        B: January 28, 1912.
        D:
        M: David Hunter,
        B: October 12, 1910.
        D:
        (Anna & Davids' children are=)
    482. Diane Lee Hunter.
        B: September 23, 1935.
        D:
        M:
        B:
        D:
    483. Judith Rae Hunter.
        B: August 22, 1937.
        D:
        M:
        B:
        D:

362. MELVIN ABERNATHY.
        B: June 28, 1914.
        D:
        M: Samuel Massey
        B: January 16, 1917.
        D:
        Samuel's and Melvins children are=
    484. Thomas Herbert Massey,
        B: April 21, 1938.
        D:
        M:
        B:
        D:
    485. Linda Lou Massey,
        B: January 31, 1941.
        D:
        M:
        B:
        D:

363. THOMAS ALEXANDER ABERNATHY, JR
        B: August 10, 1916.
        D:
        M: Edythe Whitehead,
        B: August 8, 1918.
        D:

        Tom and Edythe's children are on
        next page No. 63

363. (Continued)

Thomas & Edythe's Abernathys children:
486. Charlsie Lou Abernathy.
   B: April 21,1942.
   D:
   M:
   B:
   D:
487. Peggy Ann Abernathy.
   B: May 19, 1946.
   D:
   M:
   B:
   D:

364.

NETTIE JANE ABERNATHY.
   B: March 24, 1921.
   D:
   M: John H.Hackney,Sr.
   B: March 10, 1922.
   D:
John's and Nettie's children are:
488. John H.Hackney,Jr.
   B: December 12, 1947.
   D:
   M:
   B:
   D:
489 Thomas Kelley Hackney.
   B: May 2,1949.
   D:
   M:
   B:
   D:
490. Sally Ann Hackney.
   B: June 12, 1951.
   D:
   M:
   B:
   D:

368:

CLARA P.WELKER.
   B: March 29,1912.
   D:
   M: Albert Warner. on Sept 11,1927.
   B: December 27,1908.
   D:
Albert & Clara's children are:

491. Evelyn Maxine Warner.
   B: March 17,1928.
   D:
   M: James Richard Warner.
   B: ?
   D: ?
492: Cynthia Nadine Warner.
   B: March 24,1930.
   D:
   M: Murphy Lowell Wells.
   B: ?

See next page for their children:

64.

368 (Continued)

493: <u>Peggy Jean Warner.</u>
B: January 4, 1932.
D:
M: James Martin.
B: ?
D:

494. <u>Alberta Marie Warner.</u>
B: August 3, 1933.
D:
M: Roy Jones.
B:
D:

495. <u>Jacquelin Vivian Warner.</u>
B: June 1, 1938.
D:
M:
B:
D

496. <u>Sharon Faith Warner.</u>
B: November 28, 1946.
D:
M:
B:
D:

497. <u>Kevin Matthew Warner.</u>
B: April 27, 1951.
D:
M:
B:
D:

369.

WOODROW WILLIAM WELKER.
B: June 10, 1914.
D:
M: Mary Frances Stover, on Sept 2,
B: July 21, 1918.   1939.
D:

The children of Woodrow & Mary's are:

498. <u>James Lee Welker.</u>
B: October 24, 1940
D:
M:
B:
D:

499. <u>Marilou Kathleen Welker.</u>
B: November 9, 1952.
D:
M:
B:
D:

370.

MARY IRENE WELKER.
B: September 27, 1916.
D:
M: (1) Edward Bennett.
M: (2) Elmer Taylor.
Child by Edward & Irene Bennett is:

500. <u>Sheila Maureen Bennett.</u>
B: January 10, 1934.
D:
M: Glen Stewart.

372.   THOMAS PARKER BOWMAN.
        B: June 19, 1917.
        D:
        M: Sheila Goodall Fraser.
        B: August 6, 1921.
        D:
        Thomas and Sheila's children are:
   501. Thomas Alexander DeWitt (Tad) Bowman.
        B: July 20, 1944.
        D:
        M:
        B:
        D:
   502. Grant Fraser Bowman.
        B: March 6, 1952.
        D:
        M:
        B:
        D:
   503. David Parker Bowman.
        B: October 16, 1954.
        D:
        M:
        B:
        D:

373.   PATRICIA HAMILTON BOWMAN.
        B: April 24, 1920.
        D:
        M: Dr. Amos Johnson Shaler, D.SC.
           Head of the Department of Metal-
           lurgy, Penn State University at
           State College, Pa.
        B: July 8, 1917.
        D:
        Amos & Patricia Shaler's children are:
   504. Louise Shaler.
        B: November 10, 1947.
        D:
        M:
        B:
        D:
   505. Cynthia Shaler.
        B: October 6, 1949.
        D:
        M:
        B:
        D:
   506. James Lane Shaler.
        B: March 21, 1954.
        D:
        M:
        B:
        D:

375. PAUL HOOVER BOWMAN:
       B: June 20, 1914.
       D:
       M: Evelyn Stauffer.
       B:
       D:
       Paul and Evelyn's children are:
   507. Richard Scott Bowman.
        B: December 8, 1943.
        D:
        M:
        B:
        D:
   508. Marilyn Bowman, (Adopted)
        B: September 14, 1948.
        D:
        M:
        B:
        D:
   509. Douglas W. Bowman, (Adopted)
        B: November 16, 1954.
        D:
        M:
        B:
        D:
   510. Debora Kay Bowman.
        B: November 16, 1954
        D:
        M:
        B:
        D:

376. GRACE BOWMAN.
       B: October 8, 1917.
       D:
       M: Robert Koons on Jan 1, 1949.
       B: July 11, 1917.
       D:
       Robert & Grace's children are:
   511. Stephen H. Koons.
        B: February 19, 1950.
        D:
        M:
        B:
        D:
   512. Philip Alan Koons.
        B: July 21, 1951.
        D:
        M:
        B:
        D:
   513. Ann Bowman Koons.
        B: January 28, 1955.
        D:
        M:
        B:
        D:

377. JOHN EVANS BOWMAN.
        B: April 23, 1920.
        D:
        M: Virginia Kerlin, on July 10, 1945.
        B: September 4, 1920.
        D:
        John & Virginia Bowmans children:
      514. Carol Sue Bowman.
        B: March 2, 1951.
        D:
        M:
        B:
        D:
      515. Kathlyn Jo Bowman.
        B: February 28, 1953.
        D:
        M:
        B:
        D:
      516. Barbara Jean Bowman.
        B: April 6, 1956.
        D:
        M:
        B:
        D:

378. REBECCA GENE BOWMAN.
        B: January 1, 1925.
        D:
        M: Charley B. Johnson on Mar 21, 1953.
        B:
        D:
        Charley & Rebecca's children are:
      517. Rebecca Rae Johnson.
        B: March 23, 1955.
        D:
        M:
        B:
        D:

384. LOUISE BOWMAN.
        B:
        D:
        M: George Nipe.
        B:
        D:
        Their children are as follows:
      518. _____

      519. _____

      520. _____
        Have no record of these above children, maybe some one can supply them.

385. ROSA LEE BOWMAN.
        B:
        D:
        M: Hugh Moomaw:
      521. _____   No record of
                                      this one child.

68.

416.   **WILLIAM HERBERT BALDRIDGE.**
         B: August 31,1909.
         D:
         M: Margaret Carrell.
         B: June 28,1917.
         D:
         William and Margaret's childern are:

         522. <u>Robert Sam Baldridge.</u>
              B: March 23, 1951.
              D:
              M:
              B:
              D:

418:     <u>JEWELL D. PORTIS.</u>
         B: April 26, 1902.
         D:
         M: Emmett L. Heady,
         B: September 28, 1900.
         D:
         Their children are as follows:
         523. <u>Robert E. Heady.</u>
              B: October 7, 1920.
              D:
              M:
              B:
              D:
         524. <u>Ronald Lee Heady</u>
              B: September 27, 1925.
              D:
              M:
              B:
              D:

419.   <u>BESSIE ELIZABETH PORTIS.</u>
         B: May 2, 1907.
         D:
         M: Roy Fox.
         B:
         D:
         Their children as follows:
         525. Jerry Gene Fox.
              B: April 25, 1926.
              D:
              M:
              B:
              D:

420.   <u>AMY ELIZABETH BALDRIDGE.</u> R.N.
         B: October 20, 1911.
         D:
         M: Clifford W. Wilson, on Aug 19,
         B: January 11, 1911.   1941.
         D:
         Their chilaren are:
         526. <u>Ronald C. Wilson.</u>
              B: May 11, 1944.
              D:
              M:
              B:
              D:

69.

421.   WILLIAM JOSEPH BALDRIDGE.
         B: August 7, 1920.
         D:
         M: Geraldine V. Stoff.
         B: February 22, 1922.
         D:
         William & Geraldine Baldridge children are:
    527. William J. Baldridge.
         B: October 21, 1942.
         D:
         M:
         B:
         D:
    528. Sandra Ann Baldridge.
         B: January 11, 1948.
         D:
         M:
         B:
         D:
    529. Dennis J. Baldridge.
         B: March 24, 1954.
         D:
         M:
         B:
         D:

422.   LYMAN RUSSELL BOWMAN, JR.
         B: June 23, 1907.
         D:
         M: Lida Powell.
         B: September 17, 1907.
         D:
         Lyman and Lida's children are:
    530. Jack Powell Bowman.
         B: June 8, 1931.
         D:
         M:
         B:
         D:
    531. David Gray Bowman.
         B: November 17, 1934.
         D:
         M:
         B:
         D:

423.   KATHLEEN FORDE BOWMAN.
         B: April 23, 1909.
         D:
         M: Burnice Anderson Farmer.
         B: April 18, 1902.
         D:

         (See next page for their children)

423. (Continued)

532. Joseph Lyman Farmer.
    B: February 22, 1933.
    D:
    M:
    B:
    D:

424. BENJAMIN LEE BOWMAN.
    B: October 18, 1920.
    D:
    M: Rita Laurie Heisserer.
    B: April 15, 1920.
    D:
    Benjamin and Rita's children are:

533. Stephen Paul Bowman. (Adopted)
    B: July 17, 1948.
    D:
    M:
    B:
    D:

534. Laurie Lee Bowman. (Adopted)
    B: July 1, 1952.
    D:
    M:
    B:
    D:

426. ELIZABETH V. BOWMAN.
    B: March 7, 1915.
    D:
    M: Narcisse Edward Fuchs.
    B: August 7, 1910.
    D:
    Narcisse & Elizabeth's children are:

535. Narcisse Edward Fuchs, Jr.
    B: June 2, 1943.
    D:
    M:
    B:
    D:

536. Joseph Paul Fuchs.
    B: July 18, 1946.
    D:
    M:
    B:
    D:

537. Robert Bowman Fuchs.
    B: September 4, 1948.
    D:
    M:
    B:
    D:

538. John William Fuchs.
    B: November 25, 1952.
    D:
    M:
    B:
    D:

427. ADAGENE BOWMAN.
  B: May 20, 1917.
  D:
  M: Guy Edwin Dixon, Jr
  B: August 21, 1920.
  Guy and Adagene's children, are:
539. Margot Elizabeth Dixon.
  B: November 21, 1939,
  D:
  M:
  B:
540. Guy Edwin Dixon, 3rd
  B: February 22, 1946.
  D:
  M:
  B:

428. JOHN WEBSTER BOWMAN.
  B: August 9, 1919.
  D:
  M: Eleanor Noyes Hempstone.
  B:
  D:
  John and Eleanor's children are:
541. John Webster Bowman, Jr
  B: February 7, 1944.
  D:
  M:
  B:
  D:
542. Ellen Hempstone Bowman.
  B: May 11, 1947.
  D:
  M:
  B:
  D:
543. William Cox Bowman.
  B: September 6, 1950.
  D:
  M:
  B:
  D:

LEE AUSTIN BOWMAN.
  B: June 30, 1923.
  D:
  M: Cathleen Carpenter.
  B: June 20, 1927.
  D:
  Lee A and Cathleen's children are:
544. Camille Bowman.
  B: September 9, 1949.
  D:
  M:
  B:
  D:
545. Lee Austin Bowman, Jr
  B: July 8, 1952.
  D:
  M:
  B:
  D:
546. Marilyn Cox Bowman.
  B: December 31, 1953,
  D:

430.   SAMUEL SCHUYLER BOWMAN, JR
          B: February 5, 1945.
          D:
          M:(1) Julia Mattie Fenimore.
          B: January 21, 1915.
          D: December 21,1935.
          M: (2) Josephine Evelyn Hopper.
          B: November 23, 1915.
          D:
              Children by (1) Marriage was:
547.   Samuel Schuyler Bowman, 3rd
          B: Dec 10,1935.
          D:
          M:
          B:
          D:
              Children by the (2) Marriage is:
548.   David Paul Bowman.
          B: January 3,1948.
          D:
          M:
          B:
          D:
549.   Philip Lee Bowman.
          B: August 12, 1951.
          D:
          M:
          B:
          D:

431.   EUGENE FOWLER BOWMAN.
          B: August 3,1917.
          D:
          M: (1) RoseMary Tallent.
          B: May 6,1917.
          D:
          M: (2) Dorothy Mae Henthorn.
          B: July 27,1924.
          D:
              Children by Eugene & Rose Mary, is:
550.   Carol Jean Bowman.
          B: July 29,1937.
          D:
          M:
          B:
          D:
551:      William Morrell Bowman.
          B: August 10, 1942.
          D:
          M:
          B:
          D:
              Children by the second marriage:
552.   Dorothy Ann Bowman.
          B: April 3,1945.
          D:
          M:
          B:
          D:
              (See next page for next child.)

431 (Continued)

553. Peggy Lee Bowman.
B: August 24, 1948.
D:
M:
B:
D:

432. FRANCES EMOGENE BOWMAN.
B: February 11, 1921,
D: October 10, 1953.
M: William Henry Simmons,
B: July 7, 1923.
D:

Frances and William's child.
554. Sally Anna Simmons.
B: May 27, 1943.
D:
M:
B:
D:

433. MARGARET EMILY BOWMAN.
B: August 15, 1918.
D:
M: Cap't Robert W. Howard.
B: July 4, 1915.
D:

Robert & Margaret's children:
555. Margaret Emily Howard.
B: May 13, 1954.
D:
M:
B:
D:

434. Arnold Paul Bowman, JR.
B: September 5, 1920.
D:
M: Jean Linville Welke.
B: September 22, 1920.
D:

(Their children)
556. Mary Linville Bowman.
B: July 5, 1944.
D:
M:
B:
D:

557. Melissa Hamilton Bowman.
B: April 21, 1948.
D:
M:
B:
D:

442. MARGARET DYSART BOWMAN.
B: April 17, 1911.
D:
M: Charles Jefferson Griffith, Jr
B: January 10, 1908.
D:

442. (Continued)

74.
    Charles and Margaret Griffith's children:
558. <u>Charles Jefferson Griffith, 3rd</u>
    B: May 27, 1937.
    D:
    M:
    B:
    D
559. <u>Curtis Burette Griffith</u>.
    B: October 1, 1941.
    D:
    M:
    B:
    D:

443. CHARLES DALE BOWMAN.
    B: February 28, 1916.
    D:
    M: Sally Mable Pass.
    B: February 19, 1918.
    D:
    Charles Dale & Sally's children:
560. <u>Charles Whitener Bowman</u>.
    B: October 17, 1940.
    D:
    M:
    B:
    D:
561. <u>James Patrick Bowman</u>.
    B: November 9, 1943.
    D:
    M:
    B:
    D:

444. RUTH FRANCES BOWMAN.
    B: February 2, 1920.
    D:
    M: Jay William Miller, on Jan 21, 1944.
    B: March 9, 1913.
    D:
    Ruth Frances & Jay's Children.
562. <u>Jay William Miller, Jr</u>.
    B: May 31, 1946.
    D:
    M:
    B:
    D:
563. <u>Phillip Dale Miller</u>.
    B: May 15, 1949.
    D:
    M:
    B:
    D:

445. BYRON BURETTE BOWMAN.
    B: November 1, 1923.
    D:
    M: Lethea Ann Davis.
    B: February 24, 1927.
    D:
    (Their children on next page)

445. (Continued)
     75.
      Byron & Lethea's Children:
    564. Teresa Ann Bowman.
      B: November 11,1949.
      D:
      M:
      B:
      D:

    565. Melinda Sue Bowman.
      B: September 8, 1954.
      D: AUG 6 1956
      M:
      B:
      D:

446.   <u>WILDA VIRGINIA SMYTHE</u>.
      B: October 5,1912.
      D:
      M: Cloyd Gale Abbott, on June 17,
      B: March 23,1909.   1934.
      D:
     Virginia and Dick's child is:
    566. <u>James Darwin Abbott</u>.
      B: December 19,1946.
      D:
      M:
      B:
      D:

447.   <u>MARY LEE SMYTHE</u>.
      B: February 7,1915.
      D:
      M: Frederick H. Peterson.
      B: May 8, 1914.
      D:
     Fred and Mary Lee's children are:
    567. <u>Sondra Janeane Peterson</u>.
      B: February 16,1947.
      D:
      M:
      B:
      D:
    568. <u>Richard Brent Peterson</u>.
      B: February 17, 1951
      D:
      M:
      B:
      D:

450.   <u>GEORGIA MAURINE EVANS</u>.
      B: April 29,1927.
      D:
      M: Harold Eugene Snider, Dec 3,1950.
      B: July 24, 1925.
      D:
     Harold & Georgia's children are:
    569. <u>Sandy Maurine Snider</u>.
      B: November 19,1953.
      D:
      M:
      B:
      D:

450. (Continued)

570. Cheryl Kay Snider.
B: August 19, 1955.
D:
M:
B:
D:

451.

ELIZABETH SUE (BETSY) MEEK.
B: September 4, 1918.
D:
M: George Willard Price.
B: November 20, 1914.
D:
    The children of George & Betsy:
571. Mary Price.
B: May 1, 1948.
D:
M:
B:
D:
572. James Meek Price.
B: October 23, 1953.
D:
M:
B:
D:

452.

MARY LOUISE HIGGINS.
B: January 30, 1926.
D:
M: Warren Litton Smith.
B: November 2, 1922.
D:
    Warren & Mary's Children:
573. Pamela Ann Smith.
B: February 11, 1944.
D:
M:
B:
D:
574. Linda Lou Smith.
B: March 31, 1946.
D:
M:
B:

457.

JAMES WILSON BOWMAN.
B: November 19, 1914.
D:
M: Edna Ruth Davis.
B: July 21, 1906.
    James & Edna's Children:
575. James Wilson Bowman, 2nd
B: October 15, 1939.
D:
M:
B:
576. Edna Ann Bowman.
B: September 6, 1943.
D:
M:
B:
D:

77,

458. MARGARET BOWMAN
    B: January 26, 1916.
    D:
    M: Hubert Harlice Coates
    B: September 29, 1909.
    D:
    Margaret & Hubert Coates children are:

  577. Margaret Ann Coates.
    B: September 26, 1939.
    D:
    M:
    B:
    D:

  578. Emma Jo Coates.
    B: August 23, 1945.
    D:
    M:
    B:
    D:

459. VIRGINIA LEE BOWMAN.
    B: August 2, 1925.
    D:
    M: James Henry B. Timberlake.
    B: June 11, 1924.
    D:
    James Henry & Virginia Lee's children are:

  579. Sharon Lee Timberlake.
    B: December 11, 1945.
    D:
    M:
    B:
    D:

  580. James Richard Timberlake.
    B: March 19, 1948.
    D:
    M:
    B:
    D:

461. Robert Bryce Goodwin, 2nd
    B: May 9, 1925.
    D:
    M: Carol Ann Dunn.
    B: July 15, 1928.
    D:
    Robert & Carol Ann's children are:

  581. Teresa Ann Goodwin.
    B: August 25, 1955.
    D:
    M:
    B:
    D:

462. JAMES LEE GOODWIN.
    B: January 17, 1928.
    D:
    M: Mary Ernest Clack, on June 19, 1950.
    B: September 19, 1927
    D:

462.(Continued)   The children of James & Mary Goodwin:
       582. James Lee Goodwin, 2nd
            B: September 29, 1951.
            D:
            M:
       583. Cathryn Lane Goodwin.
            B: July 10, 1953.
            D:
            M:

463.   LANE ALDEN GOODWIN.
            B: October 9, 1929.
            D:
            M: Linda Beebe.
            B: November 16, 1934
            D:
            Lane & Linda's children are:
       584. Thomas Lane Goodwin.
            B: July 30, 1954.
            D:
            M:
       584½. Kimberly Ann Goodwin.
            B: February 2, 1956.
            D:
            M:

464.   BARBARA LOUISE BOWMAN.
            B: October 7, 1927.
            D:
            M: Jay M. Axtell.
            D:
            Jay & Barbara's children are:
       585. Ronnie Axtell.
            B: January 6, 1944.
            D:
            M:
       586. Tony Lee Axtell.
            B: December 27, 1947.
            D:
            M:

465.   BENJAMIN LEE BOWMAN, Jr
            B: July 30, 1929.
            D:
            M: Sharon Kaye Harwood,
            B: June 23, 1937.
            D: Their children are:
       586½. Barry Lee Bowman.
            B: April 3, 1956.
            D:
            M:

466.   JOE ANN BOWMAN.
            B: March 3, 1931.
            D:
            M: Robert E. Miller.
            B: March 1, 1928
            Robert & Joe Ann's children are:
       587. Robert E. Miller, Jr
            B: April 8, 1954.
            D:
            M:
            B:
            D:

466. (Continued)
588. Richard Alan Miller.
B: September 23, 1955.
D:
M:
B:
D:

471.
CATHERINE ANNA BOWMAN.
B: April 27, 1930.
D:
M: Glenn Patrick Seyferth.
B: October   1929.
D:
Glenn and Catherine's children:
589. Catherine Diana Seyferth.
B: March 9, 1947.
D:
M:
B:
D:
590. Susan Elizabeth Seyferth.
B: April 2, 1950.
D:
M:
B:
D:
591. Glenn Patrick Seyferth, Jr.
B: May 10, 1953.
D:
M:
B:
D:

480.
JOHN D. McNABB, JR.
B: November 15, 1920.
D:
M: Irene Nuffer.
B: July 23, 1928.
D:
John & Irene's children are:
592. Kevin Charles McNabb.
B: July 10, 1951.
D:
M:
B:
D:
593. Mellissa Lynn McNabb.
B: September 5, 1953.
D:
M:
B:
D:

481.
FRIEDA AGNES (Peggy) NOSER.
B: July 24, 1920.
D:
M: Audrey M. Nelson.
B: December 31, 1918.
D:

481. (Continued)

594. Joe Lee Nelson.
    B: January 8, 1943.
    D:
    M:
    B:

594½. Vickie Lynn Nelson.
    B: January 3, 1950.
    D:
    M:
    B:

491. EVELYN MAXINE WARNER.
    B: March 17, 1928.
    D:
    M: James Richard Warner.
    B:
    James and Evelyn's children are:

595. Rita Christine Warner.
    B: October 13, 1953.
    D:
    M:
    B:

596. Paula Gayle Warner.
    B: 1955.
    D:
    M:

492. CYNTHIA NADINE WARNER.
    B: March 24, 1930.
    D:
    M: Murphy Lowell Wells,
    B:
    D:
    Murphy and Cynthia's children are:

597. Ernest Wells
    B: February 22, 1951.
    D:
    M:
    B:

598. Thomas Wells
    B: December 25, 1951.
    D:
    M:
    B:

599. Arthur Wells.
    B: 1952.
    D:
    M:
    B:

600. Betty Ann Wells.
    B: 1952.
    D:
    M:
    B:
    D:

601. Kathleen Wells.
    B: 1955.
    D:
    M:
    B:
    D:

81.

493. PEGGY JEAN WARNER.
      B: January 4, 1932.
      D:
      M: James Martin.
      B: ?
      D:
      James & Peggy's children are:
   602. Alberta Thomas Martin.
        B:
        D:
        M:
        B:
        D:
   603. David Gerald Martin.
        B: 1949.
        D:
        M:
        B:
        D:
   604. Patricia Ann Martin.
        B: 1952.
        D:
        M:
        B:
        D:
   605. Barbara Ann Martin.
        B: 1953.
        D:
        M:
        B:
        D:
   606. Loretta Lynn Martin.
        B: 1955.
        D:
        M:
        B:
        D:
        (All the above children were born at Bessville, Missouri.)

494. ALBERTA MARIE WARNER.
      B: August 3, 1933.
      D:
      M: Roy Jones.
      B: ?
      D:
      Roy and Alberta's children are:
   607. Bryan Douglas Jones.
        B.   1955.
        D:
        M:
        B:
        D:

500. SHEILA MAUREEN BENNETT.
      B: January 10, 1934.
      D:
      M: Glen Stewart.
      B:
      D:
      Glen & Sheila's children on next page #82.

500. (Continued)   608. Glenda June Stewart.
                        B: 1954.
                        D:
                        M:
                        B:
                        D:

                   609. Mildred Stewart.
                        B: 1955
                        D:
                        M:
                        B:
                        D:

Section - B

This section covers a descriptive record together with some Biographies, and A uto-Biographies of the writers paternal grand father, and his descendants down to the present day October 1956.

We had hopes of obtaining a large number of Biographies, as well as Auto-Biographies, but only a few came in.

However the Index will give interesting information as to addresses and vocations of those of the present time.

This section no doubt should be interesting to those of the present generation.

We would be pleased to have any comment from those who may receive a copy of this history, or those who may by chance have an opportunity to look one over.

This history can be found in the Library of The Institute of American Genealogy, 407 South Dearborn Street, Chicago 5, Illinois.

B.W.Bowman,

B.W.Bowman, Historian
Address: Eudora, Arkansas.

BOWMAN GENEALOGY

Descendants of

BENJAMIN BOWMAN, 1804 AND SOPHIA FERGUSON, 1805

FATHER: BENJAMIN LEE BOWMAN,
- BORN: IN FRANKLIN COUNTY, VIRGINIA.
- DATE: JANUARY 31, 1837.
- DIED: MARCH 3, 1920.

MOTHER: ELIZA JANE FORD.
- BORN: PUTNAM COUNTY, VIRGINIA.
- DATE: FEBRUARY 21, 1840.   Married Oct 6, 1856.
- DIED: JUNE 25, 1930.   at Oak Ridge, Mo.

===

THEIR CHILDREN

DAUGHTER: AMY SOPHIA,
- BORN: IN CAPE GIRARDEAU COUNTY, MISSOURI.
- DATE: SEPTEMBER 23, 1857.
- DIED: MAY 18, 1899.

SON: WILLIAM CHESLEY,
- BORN: IN CAPE GIRARDEAU COUNTY, MISSOURI.
- DATE: SEPTEMBER 27, 1859.
- DIED: APRIL 22, 1950.

SON: CHARLES CHRISTOPHER,
- BORN: IN CAPE GIRARDEAU COUNTY, MISSOURI.
- DATE: SEPTEMBER 4, 1861.
- DIED: FEBRUARY 4, 1906.

DAUGHTER: MARY LEE,
- BORN: IN CAPE GIRARDEAU COUNTY, MISSOURI.
- DATE: OCTOBER 20, 1863.
- DIED: (IN INFANCY)   (Continued to next page)

(Continued from Page 101.)

BOWMAN GENEALOGY
Descendants of

BENJAMIN BOWMAN, and SOPHIA FERGUSON
1804 1805

DAUGHTER: NETTIE,
- BORN: CAPE GIRARDEAU COUNTY, MISSOURI.
- DATE: JUNE 19, 1866.
- DIED: FEBRUARY 4, 1948.

SON: SAMUEL LEE,
- BORN: IN CAPE GIRARDEAU COUNTY, MISSOURI.
- DATE: SEPTEMBER 11, 1868.
- DIED: JULY 6, 1949.

SON: JAMES REED
- BORN: IN CAPE GIRARDEAU COUNTY, MISSOURI.
- DATE: OCTOBER 21, 1870.
- DIED:

SON: THOMAS FORD,
- BORN: IN CAPE GIRARDEAU COUNTY, MISSOURI.
- DATE: NOVEMBER 6, 1872.
- DIED: DECEMBER 27, 1935.

DAUGHTER: LOU ELLA,
- BORN: MARBLE HILL, BOLLINGER COUNTY MISSOURI.
- DATE: JANUARY 13, 1875.
- DIED: (IN INFANCY) November 23, 1878.

SON: JOSEPH MAPLE,
- BORN: MARBLE HILL, BOLLINGER COUNTY, MISSOURI.
- DATE: JUNE 12, 1877.
- DIED: JANUARY 31, 1952.

(Continued from page 102.) 102-A

BOWMAN GENEALOGY

Descendants of

BENJAMIN BOWMAN AND **SOPHIA FERGUSON**
1804   1805

SON: WILBUR TALLEY,
   BORN: MARBLE HILL, BOLLINGER COUNTY, MISSOURI
   DATE: DECEMBER 22, 1878.
   DIED: JUNE 29, 1940.

DAUGHTER: ANNA,
   BORN: MARBLE HILL, BOLLINGER COUNTY, MISSOURI
   DATE: OCTOBER 20, 1880.
   DIED: AUGUST 1, 1955.

SON: FRANKLIN,
   BORN: MARCH 14, 1884.
   DATE: MARBLE HILL, BOLLINGER COUNTY, MISSOURI
   DIED: (IN INFANCY)

THE BIOGRAPHY OF BENJAMIN LEE BOWMAN

The Rev. Benjamin Lee Bowman was the sixth child of Benjamin and Sophia Ferguson. He was born January 31, 1837, in Franklin County Virginia, where he grew to youth.
He tried various occupations, such as Blacksmith, and a machinis but did not like any of them. So he decided to run away and become a sailor. But after reaching a port, and enlisting he became sick, and did not go to sea.

He returned home, after visiting some relatives in eastern Virginia, and then slipped off again and came to Missouri, by following some neighbors who came west.

Here he met and married Miss Eliza Ford on October 6, 1856, and settled down. The next year he induced the family to follow him to Missouri.
He possessed the faculty of being able to do almost anything he set out to do. He was a good entertainer, could imitate a negro to perfection, and was an expert banjo player.

(Continued on next page 103)

(Continued from page 102.)   102-A

BOWMAN GENEALOGY
Descendants of
BENJAMIN BOWMAN AND SOPHIA FERGUSON
1804   1805

SON: WILBUR TALLEY,

    BORN: MARBLE HILL, BOLLINGER COUNTY, MISSOURI

    DATE: DECEMBER 22, 1878.

    DIED: JUNE 29, 1940.

DAUGHTER: ANNA,

    BORN: MARBLE HILL, BOLLINGER COUNTY, MISSOURI

    DATE: OCTOBER 20, 1880.

    DIED: AUGUST 1, 1955.

SON: FRANKLIN,

    BORN: MARCH 14, 1884.

    DATE: MARBLE HILL, BOLLINGER COUNTY, MISSOURI

    DIED: (IN INFANCY)

THE BIOGRAPHY OF
BENJAMIN LEE BOWMAN

The Rev. Benjamin Lee Bowman was the sixth child of Benjamin and Sophia Ferguson. He was born January 31, 1837, in Franklin County Virginia, where he grew to youth.
He tried various occupations, such as Blacksmith, and a machinis but did not like any of them. So he decided to run away and become a sailor. But after reaching a port, and enlisting he became sick, and did not go to sea.

He returned home, after visiting some relatives in eastern Virginia, and then slipped off again and came to Missouri, by following some neighbors who came west.

Here he met and married Miss Eliza Ford on October 6, 1856, and settled down. The next year he induced the family to follow him to Missouri.
He possessed the faculty of being able to do almost anything he set out to do. He was a good entertainer, could imitate a negro to perfection, and was an expert banjo player.

(Continued on next page 103)

BOWMAN GENEALOGY
Descendants of
BENJAMIN BOWMAN and SOPHIA FERGUSON
1804   1805

The Biography of Benjamin Lee Bowman, (Continued)

When the Civil War came on he organized a Company, and went to the Confederate service. Captain Bowman was very popular, and was given Command of a Battery of Light Artillery, and saw some exciting service. Captain Bowman was very popular with his men because of his social qualities. And had circumstances permited he would have risen to more honorable positions. But his health could not stand the strenous service, so he resigned his Commission and came home.

He soon found that he could not stay unmolested, and was finally induced to take clerical service in the Quarter Master's department of the Federal Army.

After the war he turned Shoemaker, at which he was a success. Then later on he took up Carpentry, and Contracting. Then he turned his attention to Architecture, in each of which he excelled.

When he was about thirty years of age he was converted, and was baptized by the Elder Read and soon went to preaching, to the great delight of all the family.

In 1877 he moved to Marble Hill, Missouri, and preached for churches, and did District and State Mission work for the Baptist denomination. He was induced to serve as Justice of the Peace, which he did successfully for years. And until he became too feeble to do the work.

For years he suffered from palsy, which necessitated his early retirement from all public life.

One of his best works, and accomplishments was the building of the High, and Grammar School buildings at Dexter, Missouri back in the early 1900's.

His last years were spent in Sikeston, Missouri where he and his wife Eliza Jane had every convenience and comfort, furnished largely by his oldest son William Chesley, who was known around Sikeston as Judge Bowman.

He was for many years an active Mason, and until feebleness prevented, attended the meetings of the Grand Lodge each year.

To he and Eliza Jane were born thirteen children, three of whom died in infancy.

By Rev, Thomas A. Bowman,

BOWMAN   GENEALOGY
Descendants   of

BENJAMIN LEE BOWMAN AND ELIZA JANE FORD.
         1837   1840

FATHER: ROBERT BALDRIDGE.

    BORN: KNOXVILLE, TENNESSEE.

    DATE: FEBRUARY 4, 1834.

    DIED: DECEMBER 11, 1895.

MOTHER: AMY SOPHIA BOWMAN.

    BORN: IN CAPE GIRARDEAU COUNTY, MISSOURI.

    DATE: SEPTEMBER 23, 1857.

    DIED: MAY 18, 1899.

===
THEIR CHILDREN.

SON: HERBERT,

    BORN: POCAHONTAS, MISSOURI.

    DATE: JULY 28, 1879.

    DIED: DECEMBER 5, 1947.

DAUGHTER: IRENE;

    BORN: POCAHONTAS, MISSOURI.

    DATE: AUGUST 26, 1881.

    DIED: AUGUST 20, 1943.

SON: ROBERT LEE,

    BORN: POCAHONTAS, MISSOURI.

    DATE: JUNE 30, 1889.

    DIED:

BOWMAN GENEALOGY
Descendants of
ROBERT BALDRIDGE, 1834, ~ AMY SOPHIA BOWMAN, 1857

FATHER: HERBERT BALDRIDGE,
    BORN: POCAHONTAS, MISSOURI.
    DATE: JULY 28, 1879.
    DIED: DECEMBER 5, 1947
    MARRIED: SEPTEMBER 3, 1908 at Windsor, Ill.

MOTHER: MARY ELLEN STORM,
    BORN: ASH GROVE TOWNSHIP, ILLINOIS.
    DATE: MARCH 30, 1882.

THEIR CHILDREN

SON: WILLIAM HERBERT,
    BORN: FARMINGTON, MISSOURI.
    DATE: AUGUST 31, 1909.
    DIED:

SON: JOHN HAROLD,
    BORN: POCAHONTAS, MISSOURI.
    DATE: FEBRUARY 19, 1913.
    DIED: JULY 12, 1943.

BOWMAN   GENEALOGY
Descendants   of
HERBERT BALDRIDGE, 1879 and MARY ELLEN STORM, 1882

FATHER: WILLIAM HERBERT BALDRIDGE,
    BORN: FARMINGTON, MISSOURI.
    DATE: AUGUST 31, 1909.
    DIED:
    MARRIED: FEBRUARY 12,1938 at TOLEDO, ILL.

MOTHER: MARGARET B. CARRELL,
    BORN: GREENUP, ILLINOIS.
    DATE: JUNE 28, 1917.
    DIED:
    VOCATION: SCHOOL TEACHER.

+===+

THEIR CHILDREN

SON: ROBERT SAM,
    BORN: ELGIN, ILLINOIS.
    DATE: MARCH 23, 1951.
    DIED:

BOWMAN GENEALOGY

BIOGRAPHY
of

William Herbert Baldridge, and Margaret Kathryn Carrell

William Herbert Baldridge was born on August 31, 1909 at Farmington, Missouri, and moved to Windsor, Illinois in 1918.
He attended school at the Elm Flat Rural Grade School, and graduated at Windsor Community High School in 1929.

He then attended the University of Illinois from 1930-1931, worked as Dairy Herd Improvement Tester 1931 to 1939 in Will County Illinois, Was Herd Manager for the Pomeroy Farms, Barrington, Illinois 1939-1940, Herd Manager of Ridglydale Farms, Decatur, Illinois 1941-1944; Manager and Vice-President The Mullady Farms, in Elgin, Illinois 1944-1953; now operating his own Hampshire Swine Herd at Greenup, Illinois since 1953.

His Show herds have been consistent winners all over the United States, and breeding animals have been sold into each of the forty eight (48) States of the Union, including Canada, Cuba, Mexico, Italy, and Alaska.

At the present writing he is a Director of the Illinois Hampshire Swine Breeders' Association, and the Illinois Purebred Livestock Breeders Association.

Herb has done an outstanding job in the breeding of pure bred swine, and Livestock.

Some of the excellent results of his Hampshire breedings are CARMEN JANE 1947-1948 Illinois GRAND CHAMPION; LOCHINVAR LENA 1950 ALL AMERICAN Champion; LOCHINVAR LILL 1951 Illinois GRAND CHAMPION; LOCHINVAR QUEEN 1952 ALL AMERICAN CHAMPION.

With 65 STATE FAIR CHAMPIONS, and 52 ALL AMERICANS since 1940 speaks for itself, without a doubt.
Truly an excellent record, and a GRAND Producer.
He is known Nation Wide as a producer of FINE Swine, "WHERE INDIVIDUALITY REIGNS SUPREME." Hats off to Herb.

He married Margaret Kathryn Carrell, of Greenup, Illinois on February 12, 1938. She was born at Greenup, Illinois on June 28, 1917. She graduated from Greenup High School in 1932, attended Eastern Illinois State Teachers College in 1932-1935. A Son Robert Sam was born to them March 23, 1951. She taught school.

Any of his relatives who may be traveling in or near the vicinity of Greenup, Illinois would do well to drive by, and look Herb, and his family up, and pay them a surprise visit. I am sure it would be worth while.

By, Byron W. Bowman.

BOWMAN GENEALOGY

Descendants of
HERBERT BALDRIDGE AND MARY ELLEN STORM
1879   1882

FATHER: JOHN HAROLD BALDRIDGE,

        BORN: POCAHONTAS, MISSOURI.

        DATE: FEBRUARY 19, 1913

        Married: Long Beach, California, 1933.

        Vocation: C.P.O. Was a deep sea diver, death caused by the enemy at Gaudacanal at Henderson Flying Field.

        DIED: JULY 12, 1943.

MOTHER: ESTELLA MILLS,

        BORN: IN CALIFORNIA.

        DATE: UNKNOWN, but about 1914.

        DIED:

               NO CHILDREN

BOWMAN GENEALOGY
Descendants of
ROBERT BALDRIDGE AND AMY SOPHIA BOWMAN
1834   1857

FATHER: SAMUEL FOLSOM PORTIS,
- BORN: MARBLE HILL, MISSOURI.
- DATE: NOVEMBER 2, 1873
- DIED: Aug 18, 1929

MOTHER: IRENE BALDRIDGE
- BORN: POCAHONTAS, MISSOURI.
- DATE: AUGUST 26, 1881.
- DIED: AUGUST 20, 1943.

==

+ THEIR CHILDREN +

DAUGHTER: JEWELL D,
- BORN: POCAHONTAS, MISSOURI.
- DATE: APRIL 26, 1902.
- DIED:

DAUGHTER: BESSIE ELIZABETH,
- BORN: JACKSON, MISSOURI.
- DATE: MAY 2, 1907.
- DIED:

BOWMAN GENEALOGY

Descendants of

SAMUEL FOLSOM PORTIS   AND   IRENE BALDRIDGE
    1873   1881

FATHER: EMMETT L. HEADY,

        BORN: INDIANAPOLIS, INDIANA

        DATE: SEPTEMBER 28, 1900.

        DIED:

Present address: 4002 Lexington Ave, St Louis, Mo.

MOTHER: JEWELL D. PORTIS,
        BORN: POCAHONTAS, MISSOURI.

        DATE: APRIL 26, 1902

        DIED:
Present address: 4002 Lexington Avenue, St Louis, Mo.

+===

THEIR CHILDREN

SON: ROBERT E.

        BORN: ST LOUIS, MISSOURI.

        DATE: OCTOBER 7, 1920.

        DIED:
Present address: 330 Nowland Ave, Peoria, Ill.

SON: RONALD LEE

        BORN: ST LOUIS, MISSOURI.

        DATE: SEPT 27, 1925.

Present Address: 4002 Lexington Ave, St Louis, Mo.

BOWMAN GENEALOGY
Descendants of

SAMUEL FOLSOM PORTIS   AND   IRENE BALDRIDGE
         1873   1881

FATHER: ROY FOX
   BORN: JACKSON, MISSOURI
   DATE: SEPTEMBER 4, 1892.
   DIED:

MOTHER:
MOTHER: BESSIE ELIZABETH PORTIS.
   BORN: JACKSON, MISSOURI.
   DATE: MAY 2, 1907.
   DIED:

THEIR CHILDREN

SON: JERRY GENE,
   BORN: CAPE GIRARDEAU, MISSOURI.
   DATE: APRIL 25, 1926.
   DIED:

         Present address: Kansas City, Missouri.

BOWMAN GENEALOGY
Descendants of
ROBERT BALDRIDGE   AND   AMY SOPHIA BOWMAN
1834   1857

FATHER: ROBERT LEE BALDRIDGE.

    BORN: POCAHONTAS, MISSOURI

    DATE: JUNE 30, 1889.

    Married; January 24, 1910.

    DIED:

    Present address: 4948 Page Blvd, St Louis, Mo.

MOTHER: ALICE ELIZABETH LALUMENDIER.

    BORN: VALLEY FORGE, MISSOURI.

    DATE: APRIL 30, 1885.

    Married: January 24, 1910.

    Present address: 4948 Page Blv'd, St Louis, Mo.

+==+

THEIR CHILDREN

DAUGHTER: AMY ELIZABETH

    BORN: ST LOUIS, MISSOURI

    DATE: OCTOBER 20, 1911.

    DIED:

SON: WILLIAM JOSEPH,

    BORN: ST LOUIS, MISSOURI.

    DATE: AUGUST 7, 1920

    Died;

    Present address: In Air Force at Okanawa 8/20/1954.

BOWMAN   GENEALOGY

Descendants of

ROBERT LEE BALDRIDGE   AND   ALICE ELIZABETH LALUMENDIER
            1889   1885

FATHER: CLIFFORD W. WILSON,

    BORN: SPARTA, ILLINOIS

    DATE: JANUARY 11, 1911

    Married: AUGUST 19, 1941

    DIED:

MOTHER: AMY ELIZABETH BALDRIDGE

    BORN: ST LOUIS, MISSOURI,

    DATE: OCTOBER 20, 1911

    Married: AUGUST 19, 1941

    Present address 4948 Page Blv'd, St Louis, Mo.

    DIED:

+==+
+ THEIR CHILDREN +

SON: RONALD C,

    BORN: ST LOUIS, MISSOURI.

    DATE: MAY 11, 1944.

    DIED:

BOWMAN GENEALOGY

Descendants of
ROBERT LEE BALDRIDGE AND ALICE ELIZABETH LALUMENDIER
1889   1885

FATHER: WILLIAM JOSEPH BALDRIDGE,

     BORN: ST LOUIS, MISSOURI

     DATE: AUGUST 7, 1920

     Married: August 31, 1941

       Died:

MOTHER: GERALDINE V. STOFF,

     BORN: ST LOUIS, MISSOURI

     DATE: FEBRUARY 22, 1922

     DIED:

+==+

+THEIR CHILDREN +

SON: WILLIAM J,

     BORN: ST LOUIS, MISSOURI

     DATE: OCTOBER 21, 1942

     DIED:

DAUGHTER: SANDRA ANN,

     BORN: ST LOUIS, MISSOURI

     DATE: JANUARY 11, 1948

     DIED:

SON: DENNIS J,

     BORN: FALMOUTH, MASSACHUSETTS.

     DATE: MARCH 24, 1954

     DIED:

BOWMAN   GENEALOGY

Descendants   of

BENJAMIN LEE BOWMAN AND ELIZA JANE FORD
             1837   1840

FATHER: WILLIAM CHESLEY BOWMAN,
    BORN: IN CAPE GIRARDEAU COUNTY, MISSOURI,
    DATE: SEPTEMBER 27, 1859
    DIED: APRIL 22, 1950

MOTHER: EMMA ESTES,
    BORN: IN BOLLINGER COUNTY, NEAR BURFORDVILLE, MO.
    DATE: FEBRUARY 1, 1864
    DIED: JANUARY 5, 1938

+ === +
              + THEIR CHILDREN +

SON: LYMAN RUSSELL,
    BORN: BURFORDVILLE, MISSOURI,
    DATE: OCTOBER 12, 1883
    DIED:

DAUGHTER: EULA CLIPPARD,
    BORN: BURFORDVILLE, MISSOURI.
    DATE: NOVEMBER 11, 1885
    DIED:

SON: JOSEPH,
    BORN: JACKSON, MISSOURI
    DATE: JANUARY 3, 1889
    DIED:

SON: LEE REED,
    BORN: BURFORDVILLE, MISSOURI
    DATE: JANUARY 25, 1891.
    DIED:

BOWMAN GENEALOGY

Descendants of

BENJAMIN LEE BOWMAN AND ELIZA JANE FORD,
1840
(Continued from page 114)

SON: SAMUEL SCHUYLER,
    BORN: BURFORDVILLE, MISSOURI,
    DATE: MAY 13, 1893
    DIED:

SON: ARNOLD PAUL,
    BORN: SIKESTON, MISSOURI
    DATE: FEBRUARY 15, 1896
    DIED: FEBRUARY 7, 1948

SON: ROBERT BYRON,
    BORN: SIKESTON, MISSOURI
    DATE: FEBRUARY 27, 1899
    DIED:

DAUGHTER: MELVIN EMOGENE,
    BORN: SIKESTON, MISSOURI
    DATE: MAY 26, 1901
    DIED:

DAUGHTER: MILDRED REBECCA,
    BORN: SIKESTON, MISSOURI
    DATE: DECEMBER 23, 1903
    DIED:

SON: WILLIAM CHESLEY, Jr
    BORN: SIKESTON, MISSOURI
    DATE: JULY 21, 1907
    DIED:

BOWMAN — GENEALOGY
Descendant of
BENJAMIN BOWMAN AND SOPHIA FERGUSON
1804 — 1805

BIOGRAPHY OF
WILLIAM CHESLEY BOWMAN
1859
(Page 101)

William Chesley Bowman was born on September 27, 1859 at Oak Ridge, Cape Girardeau County, Missouri. He was the second child of Benjamin Lee, and Eliza Jane Bowman.
He was the founder of The Scott County Milling Co in Sikeston, Missouri in the year 1904.
He was the fourth in a line of flour millers in the United States, and had been active in the operation of The Scott County Milling Co until just a few days before his death. In fact he was in his office at his desk on Thursday preceding his passing.

He with his grand father Benjamin Bowman, and his Uncle Samuel Sterling Bowman all millers at one time, entered the milling industry at Burfordville, Missouri., where his Uncle Samuel Bowman, was manager of a water driven mill.

While working at the Burfordville mill, he met and married Miss. Emma Estes, whom preceded him in death on January 5th, 1938 at Sikeston, Missouri.

Before moving to Sikeston in 1893 with his family, he worked for a period in the Pacific Northwest and was also a miller in Jackson, Missouri., for two years. When the family moved to Sikeston, he became associated with The Greer-Holley Milling Co., then owned by G.B. Greer, and U.G. Holley.

Later he became a partner in the Company and the name was changed to the Greer-Eberdt Milling Co. Later he sold his interest in this company and became associated with his brother Charles and other associates in purchasing the Albert Jorndt Roller Mill at Dexter, Missouri, and operating as the Dexter Milling Company, this being in the early 1900.

Some few years later he was induced by his friend Charles D. Matthews of Sikeston, Missouri to organize a new flour mill at Sikeston, and known as The Bowman-Matthews Milling Co., the name was changed to The Scott County Milling Co, with the consolidation of the Oran mill, together with the Greer-Eberdt Milling Co of Sikeston. A little later the Dexter Milling Company was merged with the Scott County Milling Co, thus resulting in the formation of a large and going industry for south-east Missouri. A company known throughout the South for its fine products, and its high standard of business integrity. Mostly due to the high standard of business policies of Uncle Billie Bowman and his posterity.

BIOGRAPHY OF
WILLIAM CHESLEY BOWMAN
1859
(Continued)

From page 115-A

He was active not only in the milling Industry, but was active in civic affairs, and at the time of his death was the "first Citizen" of Sikeston. From 1912 to 1916, he was a member of the Scott County Court, hence the title of "JUDGE" was given him. For fifteen years he was a member of the citys Board of Education, serving as President of that organization part of the time. He was a member of the Scottish Rite Masons.

In his later years he was fond of walking through the city and was a familiar figure to most Sikestonians. Besides his milling interests he was also active in live stock, and wheat production on his farms in the county.

He was long a member, and Deacon of the First Baptist Church in Sikeston. He had contributed more than half the original cost of the erection of the church building.

At the time of his death he was the tenth of a family of thirteen children to pass away. And at this writing only one brother of the very large family survives him, and that is James Reed Bowman, of Jackson, Missouri.

He passed away at the Missouri Delta Community Hospital in Sikeston, Missouri on Saturday April 22, 1950, and interment was in Sikeston Mausoleum where his good wife also lies at rest.

It is so easy to say, he was truly a great character in the Community which he resided most of his life, a lover of his Lord and Master, and he loved, and suported his church admirably.

Never have I heard a finer, and more fitting eulogy of a person, than that spoken of him by his pastor, in conducting his last funeral rites on the day he was laid to rest

By. Byron W. Bowman,
(Page 138)

BOWMAN GENEALOGY

Descendants of

WILLIAM CHESLEY BOWMAN and **EMMA ESTES,**
1859   1864

FATHER: LYMAN RUSSELL BOWMAN,
- BORN: BURFORDVILLE, MISSOURI.
- DATE: OCTOBER 12, 1883
- DIED:

MOTHER: HITA CLAUDIA GILBREATH,
- BORN: JULY 1, 1887.
- PLACE: SIKESTON, MISSOURI,
- DIED: July 15, 1954

+===================================+
+ THEIR CHILDREN +

SON: LYMAN RUSSELL, Jr
- BORN: SIKESTON, MISSOURI
- DATE: JUNE 23, 1907
- DIED:

DAUGHTER: KATHLEEN FORDE,
- BORN: SIKESTON, MISSOURI
- DATE: APRIL 23, 1909
- DIED:

SON,   BENJAMIN LEE,
- BORN: SIKESTON, MISSOURI
- DATE: OCTOBER 18, 1920
- DIED:

BOWMAN   GENEALOGY

Descendants of

LYMAN RUSSELL BOWMAN, Sr   AND   HITA CLAUDIA GILBREATH
　　　　1883　　　　　　　　　　　　　　　　1887

FATHER:　　　　　LYMAN RUSSELL BOWMAN, Jr
　　　BORN:　　SIKESTON, MISSOURI
　　　DATE:　　JUNE 23, 1907
　　　DIED:

MOTHER:　　　　　LIDA BELL POWELL
　　　BORN:　　PERRY, MISSOURI
　　　DATE:　　SEPTEMBER 17, 1907
　　　DIED:

+===+
　　　　　　　　+ THEIR CHILDREN +

SON:　　　　　　JACK POWELL,
　　　BORN:　　SIKESTON, MISSOURI
　　　DATE:　　JUNE 8, 1931
　　　DIED:

SON:　　　　　　DAVID GRAY,
　　　BORN:　　SIKESTON, MISSOURI
　　　DATE:　　NOVEMBER 17, 1934
　　　DIED:

BOWMAN GENEALOGY

Descendants of

LYMAN RUSSELL BOWMAN, Sr AND HIDA CLAUDIA GILBREATH
    1883   1887

FATHER: BURNICE ANDERSON FARMER
    BORN: NEAR ADAMS, IN ROBERTSON COUNTY, TENN.
    DATE: APRIL 18, 1902
    DIED:

MOTHER: KATHLEEN FORDE BOWMAN
    BORN: SIKESTON, MISSOURI
    DATE: APRIL 23, 1909
    DIED:

++ = ++

                + THEIR CHILDREN +

SON: JOSEPH LYMAN
    BORN: SIKESTON, MISSOURI
    DATE: FEBRUARY 22, 1933
    DIED:

BOWMAN GENEALOGY

Descendants of

WILLIAM CHESLEY BOWMAN AND EMMA ESTES
1859   1864

FATHER: WILLIAM THOMAS SHANKS
- BORN: NEW Madrid County, Missouri.
- DATE: MARCH 22, 1880
- DIED: AUGUST 29, 1926

MOTHER: EULA CLIPPARD BOWMAN,
- BORN: BURFORDVILLE, MISSOURI
- DATE: NOVEMBER 11, 1885
- DIED:

++ = ++

+ THEIR CHILDREN +

SON: WILLIAM THOMAS, Jr
- BORN: SIKESTON, MISSOURI
- DATE: NOVEMBER 25, 1912
- DIED: MAY 24, 1914

BOWMAN GENEALOGY

Descendants of

WILLIAM CHESLEY BOWMAN AND EMMA ESTES
1859   1864

FATHER: JOSEPH BOWMAN
    BORN: JACKSON, CAPE GIRARDEAU COUNTY, MISSOURI.
    DATE: JANUARY 3, 1889
    DIED:

MOTHER: MARGARET E. VAUGHAN
    BORN: RICHWOOD, SCOTT COUNTY, MISSOURI
    DATE: SEPTEMBER 26, 1888
    DIED:

++ = ++
++ THEIR CHILDREN ++

DAUGHTER: ELIZABETH V,
    BORN: ORAN, MISSOURI
    DATE: MARCH 7, 1915
    DIED:

DAUGHTER: ADAGENE,
    BORN: ORAN, MISSOURI
    DATE: MAY 20, 1917
    DIED:

BOWMAN GENEALOGY

Descendants of

JOSEPH BOWMAN   AND   MARGARET E. VAUGHAN
    1889   1888

FATHER: NARCISSE EDWARD FUCHS
    BORN: TELL CITY, INDIANA
    DATE: AUGUST 7, 1910
    DIED:

MOTHER: ELIZABETH V. BOWMAN
    BORN: ORAN, MISSOURI
    DATE: MARCH 7, 1915
    DIED:

++ =============================== ++
                ++ THEIR   CHILDREN ++

SON: NARCISSE EDWARD, Jr
    BORN: CAPE GIRARDEAU, MISSOURI
    DATE: JUNE 2, 1943
    DIED:

SON: JOSEPH PAUL,
    BORN: CAPE GIRARDEAU, MISSOURI
    DATE: JULY 18, 1946
    DIED:

SON: ROBERT BOWMAN,
    BORN: CAPE GIRARDEAU, MISSOURI
    DATE: SEPTEMBER 4, 1948
    DIED:

SON: JOHN WILLIAM,
    BORN: CAPE GIRARDEAU, MISSOURI.
    DATE: NOVEMBER 25, 1952.
    DIED:

BOWMAN GENEALOGY

Descendants of

JOSEPH BOWMAN AND **MARGARET E. VAUGHN**
1889 1888

FATHER: GUY EDWIN DIXON, Jr
- BORN: HENDERSONVILLE, NORTH CAROLINA.
- DATE: AUGUST 21, 1920
- DIED:

MOTHER: ADAGENE BOWMAN
- BORN: ORAN, MISSOURI
- DATE: MAY 20, 1917
- DIED:

++ = = = = = = = = = = = = = = = = = = = ++
+ THEIR CHILDREN +

DAUGHTER: MARGOT ELIZABETH,
- BORN: CAPE GIRARDEAU, MISSOURI
- DATE: NOVEMBER 21, 1939
- DIED:

SON: GUY EDWIN 3rd
- BORN: MIAMI, FLORIDA.
- DATE: FEBRUARY 22, 1946
- DIED:

BOWMAN GENEALOGY
Descendants of
WILLIAM CHESLEY BOWMAN AND EMMA ESTES
1859 1864

FATHER: LEE REED BOWMAN,
- BORN: BURFORDVILLE, MISSOURI
- DATE: JANUARY 25, 1891
- DIED:

MOTHER: VERNA ESTER COX,
- BORN: DAVIS COUNTY, INDIANA.
- DATE: MARCH 21, 1897
- DIED:

++ = ++
=+ THEIR CHILDREN +=

SON: JOHN WEBSTER,
- BORN: CAIRO, ILLINOIS
- DATE: AUGUST 9, 1919
- DIED:

SON: LEE AUSTIN,
- BORN: SIKESTON, MISSOURI
- DATE: JUNE 30, 1923
- DIED:

BOWMAN GENEALOGY
Descendants of
LEE REED BOWMAN   AND   VERNA ESTER COX
1891   1897

FATHER: JOHN WEBSTER BOWMAN
   BORN: CAIRO, ILLINOIS
   DATE: AUGUST 9, 1919
   DIED:

MOTHER: ELEANOR NOYES HEMPSTONE,
   BORN: SHANGHI, CHINA
   DATE: SEPTEMBER 3, 1924.
   DIED:

+ THEIR CHILDREN +

SON: JOHN WEBSTER, Jr
   BORN: CAPE GIRARDEAU, MISSOURI
   DATE: FEBRUARY 7, 1944.
   DIED:

DAUGHTER: ELLEN HEMPSTONE,
   BORN: WASHINGTON, D.C.
   DATE: MAY 11, 1947.
   DIED:

SON: WILLIAM COX,
   BORN: ANNAPOLIS, MARYLAND
   DATE: SEPTEMBER 6, 1950.
   DIED:

   BORN: _____
   DATE: _____
   DIED: _____

BOWMAN GENEALOGY

Descendants of

LEE REED BOWMAN   AND   VERNA ESTHER COX
     1891   1897

FATHER: LEE AUSTIN BOWMAN
      BORN: SIKESTON, MISSOURI
      DATE: JUNE 30, 1923
      DIED:

MOTHER: CATHLEEN CARPENTER
      BORN: HAMBURG, IOWA
      DATE: JUNE 20, 1927
      DIED:

++ = ++

++ THEIR   CHILDREN ++

DAUGHTER: CAMILLE,
      BORN: SIKESTON, MISSOURI
      DATE: SEPTEMBER 9, 1949
      DIED:

SON: LEE AUSTIN, Jr
      BORN: SIKESTON, MISSOURI
      DATE: JULY 8, 1952
      DIED:

DAUGHTER: MARILYN COX,
      BORN: SIKESTON, MISSOURI
      DATE: DECEMBER 31, 1953
      DIED:

      _____   _____
      BORN: _____
      DATE: _____
      DIED:

BOWMAN GENEALOGY

Descendants of

WILLIAM CHESLEY BOWMAN AND   EMMA ESTES
1859   1864

FATHER: SAMUEL SCHUYLER BOWMAN
        BORN: BURFORDVILLE, MISSOURI
        DATE: MAY 13, 1893
        DIED:

MOTHER: ILLA FOWLER,
        BORN: CLINTON, KENTUCKY
        DATE: OCTOBER 7, 1894
        DIED:

++ = ++
++ THEIR CHILDREN ++

SON: SAMUEL SCHUYLER, Jr
        BORN: SIKESTON, MISSOURI
        DATE: FEBRUARY 5, 1915
        DIED:

SON: EUGENE FOWLER,
        BORN: SIKESTON, MISSOURI
        DATE: AUGUST 3, 1917
        DIED:

DAUGHTER: FRANCES EMOGENE,
        BORN: SIKESTON, MISSOURI
        DATE: FEBRUARY 11, 1921
        DIED: OCTOBER 10, 1953

BOWMAN GENEALOGY

Descendants of

SAMUEL SCHUYLER BOWMAN AND ILLA FOWLER (First Marriage)
1893   1894

FATHER: SAMUEL SCHUYLER BOWMAN, Jr
    BORN: SIKESTON, MISSOURI
    DATE: FEBRUARY 5, 1915
    DIED:

MOTHER: JULIA MATTIE FENIMORE
    BORN: BERTRAND, MISSOURI
    DATE: JANUARY 21, 1915
    DIED: DECEMBER 21, 1935

SON: SAMUEL SCHUYLER, 3rd   THEIR CHILDREN
    BORN: SIKESTON, MISSOURI
    DATE: DECEMBER 10, 1935
    DIED:

FATHER: SAMUEL SCHUYLER BOWMAN, Jr (Second Marriage.)
MOTHER: JOSEPHINE EVELYN HOPPER,
    BORN: ABBEY, SASKATCHEWAN, CANADA.
    DATE: NOVEMBER 23, 1915
    DIED:

+ THEIR CHILDREN +

SON: DAVID PAUL,
    BORN: DENVER, COLORADO
    DATE: JANUARY 3, 1948
    DIED:

SON: PHILIP LEE,
    BORN: LEWISTOWN, MONTANA
    DATE: AUGUST 12, 1951
    DIED:

BOWMAN   GENEALOGY

Descendants of

SAMUEL SCHUYLER BOWMAN   AND   ILLA FOWLER
        1893   1894

FATHER: EUGENE FOWLER BOWMAN (First Marriage)
                                    Divorced July 14, 1943
        BORN: SIKESTON, MISSOURI

        DATE: AUGUST 3, 1917

        DIED:

MOTHER: ROSEMARY TALLENT.

        BORN: CAPE GIRARDEAU, MISSOURI

        DATE: MAY 6, 1917

        DIED:
+++ = +++
            ++ THEIR CHILDREN ++

DAUGHTER: CAROL JEAN,

        Born: CAPE GIRARDEAU, MISSOURI

        DATE: JULY 29, 1937

        DIED:

SON: WILLIAM MORRELL

        BORN   SIKESTON, MISSOURI

        DATE: AUGUST 10, 1942

        DIED:

BOWMAN GENEALOGY
Descendants of
SAMUEL SCHUYLER BOWMAN AND ILLA FOWLER
1893 — 1894

SECOND MARRIAGE OF

FATHER: EUGENE FOWLER BOWMAN

    BORN: SIKESTON, MISSOURI

    DATE: AUGUST 3, 1917

    DIED:

(Second Marriage on March 24, 1944.)

MOTHER: DOROTHY MAE HENTHORN,

    BORN: GRANT, NEBRASKA

    DATE: JULY 27, 1924

    DIED:

+++ = +++

++ THEIR CHILDREN ++

DAUGHTER: DOROTHY ANN,

    BORN: SIKESTON, MISSOURI

    DATE: APRIL 3, 1945.

    DIED:

DAUGHTER: PEGGY LEE,

    BORN: SIKESTON, MISSOURI

    DATE: AUGUST 24, 1948

    DIED:

BOWMAN GENEALOGY
Descendants of
SAMUEL SCHUYLER BOWMAN AND ILLA FOWLER
1893   1894

FATHER: WILLIAM HENRY SIMMONS, Jr
       BORN: ADVANCE, MISSOURI
       DATE: JULY 7, 1923
       DIED:

MOTHER: FRANCES EMOGENE BOWMAN,
       BORN: SIKESTON, MISSOURI
       DATE: FEBRUARY 11, 1921.
       DIED: OCTOBER 10, 1953

+:THEIR CHILDREN: +

DAUGHTER: SALLY ANNA,
       DATE: MAY 27, 1943
       BORN: SIKESTON, MISSOURI
       DIED:

BOWMAN GENEALOGY

Descendants of

WILLIAM CHESLEY BOWMAN AND EMMA ESTES
        1859   1864

FATHER: ARNOLD PAUL BOWMAN
    BORN: SIKESTON, MISSOURI
    DATE: FEBRUARY 15, 1896
    DIED: FEBRUARY 7, 1948

MOTHER: MARGARET EMILY DOVER,
    BORN: FARMINGTON, MISSOURI
    DATE: APRIL 8, 1895
    DIED:

+++ =+++

++THEIR CHILDREN++

DAUGHTER: MARGARET EMILY,
    BORN: SIKESTON, MISSOURI
    DATE: AUGUST 15, 1918.
    DIED:

SON: ARNOLD PAUL, Jr
    BORN: SIKESTON, MISSOURI
    DATE: SEPTEMBER 6, 1920
    DIED:

SON: PHILLIP DOVER
    BORN: SIKESTON, MISSOURI
    DATE: NOVEMBER 16, 1926
    DIED: JULY 18, 1948.

BOWMAN GENEALOGY

Descendants of

ARNOLD PAUL BOWMAN, Sr and MARGARET EMILY DOVER
1896   1895

FATHER: Captain, ROBERT W. HOWARD,
    BORN: ROSWELL, NEW MEXICO.
    DATE: JULY 4, 1915
    DIED:

MOTHER: MARGARET EMILY BOWMAN,
    BORN: SIKESTON, MISSOURI
    DATE: AUGUST 15, 1918.
    DIED:

++ =++
++ CHILDREN ++

DAUGHTER: MARGARET EMILY,
    BORN: MELBOURNE, FLORIDA
    DATE: MAY 13, 1954.
    DIED:

BOWMAN GENEALOGY

Descendants of

ARNOLD PAUL BOWMAN   AND   MARGARET EMILY DOVER
1896   1895

FATHER: ARNOLD PAUL BOWMAN, Jr
    BORN: SIKESTON, MISSOURI
    DATE: SEPTEMBER 5, 1920
    DIED:

MOTHER: JEAN LINVILLE WELKE.
    BORN: KANSAS CITY, MISSOURI
    DATE: SEPTEMBER 22, 1920
    DIED:

+++ =+++
=++THEIR   CHILDREN ++=

DAUGHTER: MARY LINVILLE,
    BORN: San Antonio, Texas
    DATE: JULY 5, 1944
    DIED:

DAUGHTER: MELISSA HAMILTON,
    BORN: MADISON, WISCONSIN
    DATE: APRIL 21, 1948
    DIED:

——————
    BORN: _____
    DATE: _____
    DIED: _____

——————
    BORN: _____
    DATE: _____
    DIED: _____

BOWMAN GENEALOGY

Descendants of

WILLIAM CHESLEY BOWMAN AND EMMA ESTES
        1859   1864

FATHER: ROBERT BYRON BOWMAN,
    BORN: SIKESTON, MISSOURI
    DATE: FEBRUARY 27, 1899
    DIED:

MOTHER: RUBY EVANS,
    BORN: GORIN, MISSOURI
    DATE: DECEMBER 15, 1899
    DIED:

++++ = ++++

++THEIR CHILDREN++

DAUGHTER: JANE EVANS,
    BORN: SIKESTON, MISSOURI
    DATE: OCTOBER 30, 1935
    DIED:

DAUGHTER: NANCY ANN,
    BORN: SIKESTON, MISSOURI
    DATE: NOVEMBER 27, 1938
    DIED:

BOWMAN GENEALOGY

Descendants of
ROBERT BYRON BOWMAN AND RUBY EVANS
1899   1899

FATHER: HOWARD EDWARD THILENIUS, 2nd
       BORN: PERRYVILLE, MISSOURI
       DATE: DECEMBER 25, 1936
       DIED:

MOTHER: JANE EVANS BOWMAN,
       BORN: SIKESTON, MISSOURI
       DATE: OCTOBER 30, 1935
       DIED:

THEIR CHILDREN

       BORN:
       DATE:
       DIED:

       BORN:
       DATE:
       DIED:

       BORN:
       DATE:
       DIED:

BOWMAN GENEALOGY

Descendants of

WILLIAM CHESLEY BOWMAN and EMMA ESTES
        1859   1864

FATHER: MILAM LABAN LIMBAUGH,

        DATE: SEPTEMBER 23, 1902

        BORN: MARQUAND, MISSOURI

        DIED:

MOTHER: MELVIN EMOGENE BOWMAN.

        BORN: SIKESTON, MISSOURI

        DATE: MAY 26, 1901.

+++ = +++

*THEIR CHILDREN *
(None)

BOWMAN GENEALOGY

Descendants of

WILLIAM CHESLEY BOWMAN AND   EMMA ESTES
         1859   1864

FATHER: Dr. LESTER PAUL HULICK.

    BORN: ETHERLY, ILLINOIS

    DATE: MARCH 26, 1899

    Married: AUGUST 18, 1927.
    DIED: AUGUST 20, 1944.
    VOCATION: Physician and Surgeon. Mansfield, Ill.

MOTHER: MILDRED REBECCA BOWMAN.

    BORN: SIKESTON, MISSOURI.

    DATE: DECEMBER 23, 1903

    DIED:

++++= = = = = = = = = = = = = = = = = = = ++++

++THEIR CHILDREN++

SON: ROBERT BOWMAN,

    BORN: NORMAL, ILLINOIS

    DATE: JANUARY 18, 1929

    DIED:

SON: CARL WEBSTER,

    BORN: NORMAL, ILLINOIS

    DATE: JANUARY 9, 1935

    DIED:

BOWMAN GENEALOGY

Descendants of

WILLIAM CHESLEY BOWMAN   AND   EMMA ESTES
          1859   1864

FATHER: WILLIAM CHESLEY BOWMAN, Jr
   BORN: SIKESTON, MISSOURI
   DATE: JULY 21, 1907
   DIED:

MOTHER: ELLEN SANDERSON,
   BORN: MONTGOMERY, ALABAMA.
   DATE: DECEMBER 30, 1907
   DIED:

+++ = +++

+ THEIR CHILDREN +

SON: WILLIAM CHESLEY, 3rd
   BORN: MONTGOMERY, ALABAMA.
   DATE: JANUARY 16, 1934
   DIED:

SON: JOHN SANDERSON,
   DATE: NOVEMBER 22, 1935
   BORN: MONTGOMERY, ALABAMA.
   DIED:

BOWMAN GENEALOGY

Descendants of
BENJAMIN LEE BOWMAN AND ELIZA JANE FORD
1837   1840

FATHER: CHARLES CHRISTOPHER BOWMAN.
- BORN: CAPE GIRARDEAU COUNTY, MISSOURI.
- DATE: SEPTEMBER 4, 1861
- DIED: FEBRUARY 4, 1906
- MARRIED: OCTOBER 23, 1883.

MOTHER: MARTHA EMELINE WHITENER BEDFORD.
- BORN: MARQUAND, MISSOURI.   Second Marriage
- DATE: FEBRUARY 14, 1853.
- DIED: OCTOBER 14, 1935.

+++ = +++

+THEIR CHILDREN +

SON: CURTIS BURETTE,
- BORN: MARQUAND, MISSOURI.
- DATE: AUGUST 14, 1884.
- DIED: DECEMBER 12, 1953.

SON: CLAUD WHITENER,
- BORN: MARQUAND, MISSOURI.
- DATE: JULY 19, 1887.
- DIED: MARCH 12, 1891.

SON: BYRON WHITENER,
- BORN: MARQUAND, MISSOURI.
- DATE: JULY 24, 1890.
- DIED:

DAUGHTER: RUTH LEE,
- BORN: MARQUAND, MISSOURI.
- DATE: MARCH 18, 1892.

BOWMAN GENEALOGY

Descendants of
BENJAMIN LEE BOWMAN AND ELIZA JANE FORD
1837   1840

(Continued from page 138)

- **FATHER:**   CHARLES CHRISTOPHER BOWMAN, 1861

- **MOTHER:**   MARTHA EMELINE WHITENER BEDFORD, 1853

========

- **DAUGHTER:**   GOLDEN VIRGINIA.
  - **BORN:**   MARQUAND, MISSOURI.
  - **DATE:**   AUGUST 16, 1893.
  - **DIED:**

++

THE BIOGRAPHY OF
CHARLES CHRISTOPHER BOWMAN

He was born on Sep 4, 1861 in Cape Girardeau County, near Oak Ridge, Missouri. He was the third child of Benjamin Lee, and Eliza Jane Bowman.
Charles Christopher, after finishing the public schools and attending Will Mayfield College at Marble Hill, Mo., and the State Normal School at Cape Girardeau, decided to take a course in telegraphy, and entered the service of The St Louis, Iron Mountain & Southern Railroad Co, (now the Missouri Pacific R.R.) as Agent, and telegraph operator, serving for many years, principally at Marquand, Missouri., where he lived for many years. Here he married Mrs. Martha Emeline Whitener (Bedford) a young widow with one child Effie Leah Bedford. While active in church work, he was licensed to preach, after conducting services in near by churches and missions, yet he never fully entered the work of the ministry.

He was transferred by agreement to the Dexter, Mo station in September 1, 1896. Having agreed with the agent at Dexter, Mo, Mike Owens, to make the change, which was agreeable to the Railroad Co. But after a few years as agent at Dexter he resigned from railroad work to become a stock holder, and Secretary of the newly organized Dexter Milling Co, a concern which his brother William Chesley Bowman of Sikeston, Mo also became a stockholder, and official. He was a 32 degree Scottish Rite Mason, a deacon in the first Baptist Church of Dexter, Mo, a member of the city's Board of Education, a member of many civic and Fraternal organizations. He lived an exemplary life. He passed away in the Mayfield Sanatarium in St Louis, Mo Feb 4, 1906, was buried in the Dexter, Mo Cemetery, where his wife is also buried.   By his son Byron W.

BOWMAN GENEALOGY

Descendants of

CHARLES CHRISTOPHER BOWMAN AND MARTHA EMELINE WHITENER BEDFORD.
    1861   1853

FATHER: CURTIS BURETTE BOWMAN,
    BORN: MARQUAND, MISSOURI
    DATE: AUGUST 14, 1884
    MARRIED: JUNE 4, 1910.
    DIED: DECEMBER 12, 1953

MOTHER: DEE DYSART,
    BORN: De KALB, MISSOURI
    DATE: JUNE 9, 1884.
    MARRIED: JUNE 4, 1910.
    DIED:

+++ = +++

+ THEIR CHILDREN +

DAUGHTER: MARGARET DYSART,
    BORN: DEXTER, MISSOURI.
    DATE: APRIL 17, 1911.
    DIED:

BOWMAN GENEALOGY
Descendants of
CURTIS BURETTE BOWMAN AND DEE DYSART
1884 1884

FATHER: CHARLES JEFFERSON GRIFFITH, Jr
    BORN: LITTLE ROCK, ARKANSAS.
    DATE: JANUARY 10, 1908.
    DIED:

MOTHER: MARGARET DYSART BOWMAN.
    BORN: DEXTER, MISSOURI.
    DATE: APRIL 17, 1911.
    DIED:

+++ = +++

+ THEIR CHILDREN +

SON: CHARLES JEFFERSON, 3rd.
    BORN: LITTLE ROCK, ARKANSAS.
    DATE: MAY 27, 1937.
    DIED:

SON: CURTIS BURETTE,
    BORN: LAKE VILLAGE, ARK
    DATE: OCTOBER 1, 1941.
    DIED:

BOWMAN   GENEALOGY

Descendants of

CHARLES CHRISTOPHER BOWMAN   AND   MARTHA EMELINE WHITENER BEDFORD
1861   1853

FATHER: BYRON WHITENER BOWMAN.

    BORN: MARQUAND, MISSOURI.

    DATE: JULY 24, 1890.

    DIED:

    MARRIED: SEPTEMBER 16, 1914.
    (First Marriage)

MOTHER: RUTH BERNICE BLANKENSHIP.

    BORN: VANDALIA, ILLINOIS.

    DATE: AUGUST 5, 1893.

    MARRIED: SEPTEMBER 16, 1914.

    DIED: JUNE 14, 1920.

    Burial in Dexter, Missouri Cemetery.

+++ = +++

+ THEIR   CHILDREN +

SON: CHARLES DALE,

    BORN: DEXTER, MISSOURI.

    DATE: FEBRUARY 28, 1916.

    DIED:

DAUGHTER: RUTH FRANCES,

    BORN: DEXTER, MISSOURI.

    DATE: FEBRUARY 2, 1920.

    DIED:

BOWMAN GENEALOGY

Descendants of

BYRON WHITENER BOWMAN AND RUTH BERNICE BLANKENSHIP
1890   1893

FATHER: CHARLES DALE BOWMAN.
    BORN: FEBRUARY 28, 1916.
    PLACE: DEXTER, MISSOURI.
    MARRIED: Sept 11, 1939
    DIED:

MOTHER: SALLY MABLE PASS.
    BORN: FEBRUARY 19, 1918.
    PLACE: REMLAP, ALABAMA.
    DIED:

+++ = +++

+ THEIR CHILDREN +

SON: CHARLES WHITENER,
    BORN: FAIRFIELD, ALABAMA.
    DATE: OCTOBER 17, 1940.
    DIED:

SON: JAMES PATRICK,
    BORN: FAIRFIELD, ALABAMA.
    DATE: NOVEMBER 9, 1943.

BOWMAN GENEALOGY

Descendants of

BYRON WHITENER BOWMAN AND RUTH BERNICE BLANKENSHIP
1890   1893

FATHER: JAY WILLIAM MILLER.

    BORN: WACO, TEXAS.

    DATE: MARCH 9, 1913

    MARRIED: Jan 21, 1944

    DIED:

MOTHER: RUTH FRANCES BOWMAN.

    BORN: DEXTER, MISSOURI.

    DATE: FEBRUARY 2, 1920.

    DIED:

+++ = +++

+ THEIR CHILDREN +

SON: JAY WILLIAM MILLER, Jr

    BORN: HOUSTON, TEXAS.

    DATE: MAY 31, 1946.

    DIED:

SON: PHILLIP DALE,

    BORN: TULSA, OKLAHOMA.

    DATE: MAY 15, 1949.

    DIED:

BOWMAN   GENEALOGY

Descendants   of

CHARLES CHRISTOPHER BOWMAN   AND   MARTHA EMELINE WHITENER BEDFORD
                1861   1853

+ Second   Marriage +   M: January 22, 1923

FATHER: BYRON WHITENER BOWMAN.
    BORN: MARQUAND, MISSOURI.
    DATE: JULY 24, 1890.
    DIED:

MOTHER: LILLIE MAE SHEHORN.
    BORN: NEAR ESSEX, STODDARD COUNTY, MISSOURI.
    DATE: AUGUST 18, 1899.
    DIED: JUNE 5, 1952.

+++ = +++

+ THEIR   CHILDREN +

SON: BYRON BURETTE,
    BORN: MEMPHIS, TENNESSEE.
    DATE: NOVEMBER 1, 1923.
    DIED:

BOWMAN   GENEALOGY

Descendants of

BYRON WHITENER BOWMAN AND LILLIE MAE SHEHORN
          1890   1899

FATHER: BYRON BURETTE BOWMAN.
    BORN: MEMPHIS, TENNESSEE.
    DATE: NOVEMBER 1, 1923.
    DIED:

MOTHER: LETHEA ANN DAVIS.
    BORN: CABOT, ARKANSAS.
    DATE: FEBRUARY 24, 1927.
    DIED:

+++ = +++

++ THEIR   CHILDREN ++

DAUGHTER: TERESA ANN,
    BORN: LITTLE ROCK, ARKANSAS.
    DATE: NOVEMBER 11, 1949.
    DIED:

DAUGHTER: MELINDA SUE,
    BORN: LITTLE ROCK, ARKANSAS.
    DATE: SEPTEMBER 8, 1954.
    DIED:

BOWMAN GENEALOGY

Descendants of

CHARLES CHRISTOPHER BOWMAN AND MARTHA EMELINE WHITENER BEDFORD
1861   1853

FATHER: ELMER LEE SMYTHE.
    BORN: DEXTER, MISSOURI.
    DATE: SEPTEMBER 29, 1891.
    MARRIED: FEBRUARY 25, 1911.
    At Bloomfield, Missouri by Judge Tucker.
    DIED:

MOTHER: RUTH LEE BOWMAN.
    BORN: MARQUAND, MISSOURI.
    DATE: MARCH 18, 1892.
    DIED:

+++ = = = = = = = = = = = = = = = = = = = +++
            ++ THEIR   CHILDREN ++

DAUGHTER: WILDA VIRGINIA,
    BORN: DEXTER, MISSOURI.
    DATE: OCTOBER 5, 1912.
    DIED:

DAUGHTER: MARY LEE,
    BORN: DEXTER, MISSOURI.
    DATE: FEBRUARY 7, 1915.
    DIED:

BOWMAN   GENEALOGY
Descendants of
ELMER LEE SMYTHE   AND   RUTH LEE BOWMAN
   1891   1892

FATHER: CLOYD GALE ABBOTT.
    BORN: TOLEDO, OHIO.
    DATE: MARCH 23, 1909.
    DATE MARRIED: JUNE 17, 1934.
    DIED:

MOTHER: WILDA VIRGINIA SMYTHE.
    BORN: DEXTER, MISSOURI.
    DATE: OCTOBER 5, 1912.

+++ = +++
      ++ THEIR CHILDREN ++

SON: JAMES DARWIN,
    BORN: OILDALE, CALIFORNIA.
    DATE: DECEMBER 19, 1946.
    DIED:

BOWMAN   GENEALOGY

Descendants of

ELMER LEE SMYTHE   AND   RUTH LEE BOWMAN
      1891   1892

FATHER: FREDERICK H. PETERSON.

    BORN: BAKERSFIELD, CALIFORNIA.

    DATE: MAY 8, 1914.

    DATE MARRIED: MARCH 23, 1946.

MOTHER: MARY LEE SMYTHE.

    BORN: DEXTER, MISSOURI.

    DATE: FEBRUARY 7, 1915.

+++ = +++

+ THEIR CHILDREN +

DAUGHTER: SONDRA JANEANE,

    BORN: BAKERSFIEED, CALIFORNIA.

    DATE: FEBRUARY 16, 1947.

    DIED:

SON: RICHARD BRENT,

    BORN: BAKERSFIELD, CALIFORNIA.

    DATE: FEBRUARY 17, 1951.

    DIED:

BOWMAN   GENEALOGY

Descendants of

CHARLES CHRISTOPHER BOWMAN AND   MARTHA EMELINE WHITENER BEDFORD
       1861   1853

FATHER: FRANKLYN HOWLETT BELLAMY.

                 BORN: NEAR- LONDON ENGLAND.

                 DATE: APRIL 23, 1892.

                 MARRIED: SEPTEMBER 11, 1925.

                 DIED:

                      (Second Marriage)

MOTHER: RUTH LEE BOWMAN (SMYTHE).

                 BORN: MARQUAND, MISSOURI.

                 DATE: MARCH 18, 1892.

                 DIED:

                      (No children by this Marriage.)
                      (Having divorced)

BOWMAN   GENEALOGY

Descendants   of

CHARLES CHRISTOPHER BOWMAN   AND   MARTHA EMELINE WHITENER BEDFORD
            1861   1853

FATHER: JAMES CLARENCE WHITE.

    BORN: AMITY, ARKANSAS.

    DATE: MARCH 19, 1892.

    MARRIED: JULY 11, 1915.
    At Dexter, Missouri By Rev Gee.

    DIED: OCTOBER 21, 1918

MOTHER: GOLDEN VIRGINIA   BOWMAN.

    BORN: MARQUAND, MISSOURI.

    DATE: AUGUST 16, 1893.

    MARRIED: JULY 11, 1915.

    DIED:

+++ = = = = = = = = = = = = = = = = = = = +++

++ THEIR CHILDREN   +

DAUGHTER: VIRGINIA LUCILLE,

    BORN: DEXTER, MISSOURI.

    DATE: SEPTEMBER 15, 1918.

    DIED:

BOWMAN GENEALOGY
Descendants of
JAMES CLARENCE WHITE AND GOLDEN VIRGINIA BOWMAN
1892   1893

FATHER: RAY WILLIE RAINEY.

    BORN: DEXTER, MISSOURI.

    DATE: JULY 6, 1915,

    MARRIED: SEPTEMBER 15, 1940
        At Blytheville, Ark. By Rev Carpenter.
        First Baptist Church.

    VOCATION: Funeral Director.

    DIED:

MOTHER: VIRGINIA LUCILLE WHITE.

    BORN: DEXTER, MISSOURI.

    DATE: SEPTEMBER 15, 1918.

    DIED:

    Vocation: School Teacher and Licensed Embalmer.

    DIED:

+++ = +++
++ THEIR CHILDREN ++

BOWMAN GENEALOGY

Descendants of

CHARLES CHRISTOPHER BOWMAN   AND   MARTHA EMELINE WHITENER BEDFORD
            1861   1853

FATHER: GEORGE ARTHUR EVANS.

    BORN: ASHERVILLE, MISSOURI.

    DATE: SEPTEMBER 6, 1868.

    MARRIED: AUGUST 24, 1922,
         By Rev W.D.Byland,

    Vocation; Insurance Salesman.

    DIED: NOVEMBER 2, 1940.

MOTHER: GOLDEN VIRGINIA BOWMAN WHITE,

    BORN: MARQUAND, MISSOURI.

    DATE: AUGUST 16, 1893.

    VOCATION: SALES LADY.

    DIED:

+++ = +++

+ THEIR   CHILDREN +

SON: CHARLES ARTHUR,

    BORN: DEXTER, MISSOURI.

    DATE: JANUARY 27, 1924.

    DIED:

DAUGHTER: GEORGIA MAURINE,

    BORN: DEXTER, MISSOURI.

    DATE: APRIL 29, 1927.

    DIED:

BOWMAN GENEALOGY
Descendants of

GEORGE ARTHUR EVANS AND GOLDEN VIRGINIA BOWMAN WHITE
         1868   1893

FATHER: CHARLES ARTHUR EVANS.
    BORN: DEXTER, MISSOURI.
    DATE: JANUARY 27, 1924.
    MARRIED: AUGUST 6, 1948.
    VOCATION: ACCOUNTANT.
    DIED:

MOTHER: HELEN LACLEDE NICHOLS.
    BORN: WINSLOW, INDIANA.
    DATE: OCTOBER 29, 1928.
    MARRIED: AUGUST 6, 1948.
    VOCATION: School Teacher.
    DIED:

+++ = = = = = = = = = = = = = = = = = = = +++
            ++ THEIR CHILDREN ++

BOWMAN GENEALOGY

Descendants of

GEORGE ARTHUR EVANS AND GOLDEN VIRGINIA BOWMAN WHITE
1868   1893

FATHER: HAROLD EUGENE SNIDER.
    BORN: DEXTER, MISSOURI.
    DATE: JULY 24, 1925.
    MARRIED: DECEMBER 3, 1950.
    VOCATION: Farming (Dairy.)
    DIED:

MOTHER: GEORGIA MAURINE EVANS.
    BORN: DEXTER, MISSOURI.
    DATE: APRIL 29, 1927.
    DIED:

+++ = +++
                ++ THEIR   CHILDREN ++

DAUGHTER   SANDY MAURINE,
    BORN: POPLAR BLUFF, MISSOURI.
    DATE: NOVEMBER 19, 1953.
    DIED:

DAUGHTER: CHERYL KAY,
    BORN: AUGUST 19, 1955.
    WHERE:
    DIED:

BOWMAN GENEALOGY

Descendants of
BENJAMIN LEE BOWMAN AND ELIZA JANE FORD.
1837   1840

FATHER: THOMAS JOSEPH JORDAN.

    BORN: POTOSI, MISSOURI.

    DATE: MARCH 21, 1864.

    MARRIED: JUNE 29, 1891.
             At Marble Hill, Mo.

    DIED: SEPTEMBER 1, 1937.

MOTHER: NETTIE BOWMAN.

    BORN: OAK RIDGE, CAPE GIRARDEAU COUNTY, MISSOURI.

    DATE: JUNE 19, 1866.

    MARRIED: JUNE 29, 1891.

    DIED: FEBRUARY 4, 1948.

+++ = +++

:THEIR CHILDREN:

DAUGHTER: PAULINE,

    BORN: HACKETT, ARKANSAS.

    DATE: SEPTEMBER 18, 1892.

    DIED:

DAUGHTER: GERALDINE,

    BORN: MARBLE HILL, MISSOURI.

    DATE: AUGUST. 27, 1894.

    DIED:

SON: MAPLE FORD,

    BORN: DESOTO, MISSOURI.

    DATE: JULY 31, 1899.

    DIED: JANUARY 30, 1900.

BOWMAN   GENEALOGY

Descendants   of

NETTIE BOWMAN   AND   THOMAS JOSEPH JORDAN
1866   1864

FATHER: JAMES HOLMES MEEK.
    BORN: CARROLLTON, KENTUCKY.
    DATE: FEBRUARY 21, 1896.
    MARRIED: AUGUST 18, 1917.
    DIED: NOVEMBER 29, 1942.

MOTHER: GERALDINE JORDAN.
    BORN: MARBLE HILL, MISSOURI.
    DATE: AUGUST 27, 1894.
    DIED:

+++ ========================= +++
    ++ THEIR   CHILDREN ++

DAUGHTER: ELIZABETH SUE (BETSY),
    BORN: LITTLE ROCK, ARKANSAS.
    DATE: SEPTEMBER 4, 1918.
    DIED:

BOWMAN GENEALOGY

Descendants of

NETTIE BOWMAN AND THOMAS JOSEPH JORDAN
1866   1864

FATHER: GEORGE WILLARD PRICE, Jr
    BORN: LITTLE ROCK, ARKANSAS.
    DATE: NOVEMBER 20, 1914.
    MARRIED: MARCH 10, 1946. Little Rock, Ark
    DIED:

MOTHER: ELIZABETH SUE (Betsy) MEEK.
    BORN: LITTLE ROCK, ARKANSAS.
    DATE: SEPTEMBER 4, 1918.
    DATE MARRIED: MARCH 10, 1946.

+++ = +++

++ THEIR CHILDREN ++

DAUGHTER: MARY,
    BORN: LITTLE ROCK, ARKANSAS.
    DATE: MAY 1, 1948.
    DIED:

SON: JAMES MEEK,
    BORN: MORRILTON, ARKANSAS.
    DATE: OCTOBER 23, 1953.
    DIED:

BOWMAN GENEALOGY
Descendants of
BENJAMIN LEE BOWMAN AND ELIZA JANE FORD
1837   1840

FATHER: SAMUEL LEE BOWMAN.

     BORN: CAPE GIRARDEAU COUNTY, MISSOURI.
     DATE: SEPTEMBER 11, 1868.
     MARRIED: JUNE 22, 1892, AT Ironton, Mo.
     DIED: JULY 6, 1949.

MOTHER: ANNIE GHERMAN.

     BORN: MADISON COUNTY, MISSOURI.
     DATE: MARCH 25, 1871.
     DIED: MAY 18, 1927.

+++ = +++

+:THEIR CHILDREN:+

DAUGHTER: NORMA LOUESE,

     BORN: LITTLE ROCK, ARKANSAS.
     DATE: NOVEMBER 19, 1906
     DIED:

SON: EDGAR GHERMAN,

     BORN: ADVANCE, MISSOURI.
     DATE: SEPTEMBER 6, 1907.
     DIED:

SON: SAMUEL LEE, Jr

     BORN: ADVANCE, MISSOURI.
     DATE: NOVEMBER 4, 1912.
     DIED:

BOWMAN GENEALOGY
Descendants of
SAMUEL LEE BOWMAN AND ANNIE GHERMAN
1868   1871

FATHER: TED HIGGINS.
    BORN: CARLYLE, ILLINOIS.
    DATE: FEBRUARY 16, 1906.
    DIED:

MOTHER: NORMA LOUESE BOWMAN.
    BORN: NOVEMBER 19, 1906.
    AT: LITTLE ROCK, ARKANSAS.
    DIED:

+++ = +++
++ THEIR CHILDREN ++

DAUGHTER: MARY LOUESE,
    BORN: DERMOTT, ARKANSAS.
    DATE: JANUARY 30, 1926.
    DIED:

BOWMAN   GENEALOGY

Descendants of

SAMUEL LEE BOWMAN   AND   ANNIE GHERMAN
         1868   1871

FATHER: WARREN LITTON SMITH.
    BORN: SHELBYVILLE, ILLINOIS.
    DATE: NOVEMBER 2, 1922.
    DIED:

MOTHER: MARY LOUESE HIGGINS.
    BORN: DERMOTT, ARKANSAS.
    DATE: JANUARY 30, 1926.
    DIED:

+++ = +++

++ THEIR   CHILDREN ++

DAUGHTER: PAMELA ANN,
    BORN: BURLINGTON, IOWA.
    DATE: FEBRUARY 11, 1944.
    DIED:

DAUGHTER: LINDA LOU,
    BORN: BURLINGTON, IOWA.
    DATE: MARCH 31, 1946.
    DIED:

162-A

BOWMAN GENEALOGY

Descendants of

BENJAMIN LEE BOWMAN AND ELIZA JANE FORD
1837 ================ 1840

(Second Marriage). FEBRUARY 22, 1928.

FATHER: SAMUEL LEE BOWMAN.
- BORN: CAPE GIRARDEAU, MISSOURI.
- DATE: SEPTEMBER 11, 1868.
- DIED: JULY 6, 1949.
- Buried at Dermott, Arkansas.

MOTHER: EDNA MCCLOY (LEEPER)
- BORN: MONTICELLO, ARKANSAS
- DATE: APRIL 14, 1880.
- DIED: JUN 15 1956

++NO CHILDREN++

BOWMAN GENEALOGY

Descendants of

SAMUEL LEE BOWMAN. AND ANNIE GHERMAN
1868   1871

FATHER: SAMUEL LEE BOWMAN, Jr
  BORN: ADVANCE, MISSOURI.
  DATE: NOVEMBER 4, 1912.
  DIED:

MOTHER: FRANCES W. WALKER.
  BORN: FORREST CITY, ARKANSAS.
  DATE: FEBRUARY 29, 1916.
  DIED:

+++ = +++
++ THEIR CHILDREN ++

DAUGHTER: ALICE ANN,
  BORN: LAKE VILLAGE, ARKANSAS.
  DATE: DECEMBER 6, 1939.
  DIED:

SON: SAMUEL LEE, 3rd
  BORN: LAKE VILLAGE, ARKANSAS.
  DATE: OCTOBER 26, 1942.
  DIED:

SON: WILLIAM WALKER,
  BORN: LITTLE ROCK, ARKANSAS.
  DATE: OCTOBER 11, 1948.
  DIED:

BOWMAN   GENEALOGY

Descendants of

HENJAMIN LEE BOWMAN   AND   ELIZA JANE FORD
1837   1840

FATHER: JAMES REED BOWMAN
    BORN: OCTOBER 21, 1870
    PLACE: POCAHONTAS, CAPE GIRARDEAU COUNTY, MISSOURI.
    DIED:

MOTHER: LILLIE B. LIVELY,
    BORN: SEPTEMBER 17, 1873
    PLACE: STEELVILLE, ILLINOIS.
    DIED:

THEIR CHILDREN

SON: HINKLE JORDAN,
    BORN: BURFORDVILLE, MISSOURI.
    DATE: FEBRUARY 13, 1894
    DIED:

SON: RICHARD EARL,
    BORN: BURFORDVILLE, MISSOURI.
    DATE: MAY 18, 1896.
    DIED:

DAUGHTER: ANICE LILYAN,
    BORN: BURFORDVILLE, MISSOURI.
    DATE: OCTOBER 6, 1900.
    DIED:

DAUGHTER: MYRTLE MARGUERITTE,
    BORN: ADVANCE, STODDARD COUNTY, MISSOURI.
    DATE: OCTOBER 31, 1903.
    DIED:

BOWMAN   GENEALOGY
B I O G R A P H Y
of
JAMES REED BOWMAN
1 8 7 0

    James Reed Bowman, the seventh child of Benjamin Lee, and Eliza Jane Ford Bowman, was born at Pocahontas, Cape Girardeau County, Missouri on October 21, 1870.

    He spent the most of his childhood and early youth at Marble Hill, Bollinger County, Missouri, where he lived with his parents and attended school at old Mayfield-Smith Academy. Here he also became a member of the First Baptist Church, of which his father was pastor.

    In the year of 1890 he moved to the town of Burfordville, Missouri. Here he worked for his brother William Chesley, who was the Manager in charge of the Water Mill at that place; it being one of the oldest flour, and corn mills west of the Mississippi River.

    On August 30, 1892 he was married to Miss. Lillie Belle Lively, the daughter of John M, and Virginia Levitt Lively; the ceremony being performed by his Uncle the Rev. Thomas Anderson Bowman of Jackson Missouri, who was at that time the pastor of the First Baptist Church at that place.

    He and his wife Lillie established their home at Burfordville ; he having became Manager of the water mill replacing his brother William Chesley,

    During the next ten or twelve years he and his wife moved to several towns in Southeast Missouri, including Sikeston, and Advance where he was associated in the operation and management of a flour mill located at that place. Finally he moved his family back to Burfordville, and at that time he built a new home,; acquired farm lands, and managed the Burfordville mill.

    During this period of time there were four children born to bless their home; Hinkle Jordan the oldest was born at Burfordville on February 13, 1894; Richard Earl born on May 18, 1896, and Anice Lilyan born on October 6, 1900 both at Burfordville, Missouri; and Myrtle Margueritte born on October 31, 1903 at Advance Missouri.

    During the year 1912, he purchased a home in Jackson, Mo and moved his family into their new home, and took over executive management in charge of one of the mills of The Cape County Milling Company, of which he acquired a financial interest. He remained active in the operation of Mill B until the summer of 1953 when he disposed of his milling interest, and retired to a quiter life.

(Continued on next page)

BIOGRAPHY OF JAMES REED BOWMAN
1 8 7 0
(Continued)

"J.R." or JIM Bowman as he is known among his friends, and associates of the community, and who number among the many thousands of individuals, has created a friendship, of the highest confidence that hundreds of them both young, and old sought his Counsel and advice.

He served as the Mayor of Jackson for 19 years, and during his administration the city carried to completition many major improvements. He took special interest in the development and improvement not only the city's affairs, but the schools, hiways, and roads in the community.

He was made a Master Mason in the Jackson Masonic fraternity in January 1902, and in 1953 he was honored by being presented a FIFTY year Pin, by the local Masonic lodge. He is also a 32 degree Scottish Rite Mason.

At the present writing he and his good wife Lillie live at Jackson, Missouri in their home, although he recently passed his 85th birthday, and she her 82nd. They both busy themselves, he looking after his real estate interests, and her the house hold affairs. He for his age maintains a lively interest in his fine family, and community affairs.

By Byron Whitener Bowman.

BOWMAN   GENEALOGY
Descendants   of

JAMES REED BOWMAN   AND   LILLIE B. LIVELY
1870   1873

FATHER: HINKLE JORDAN BOWMAN,

    BORN: BURFORDVILLE, CAPE GIRARDEAU COUNTY, MISSOURI.

    DATE: FEBRUARY 13, 1894.

    DIED:

MOTHER: LILLIAN ALMA PAPE,

    BORN: CAPE GIRARDEAU, MISSOURI.

    DATE: JANUARY 21, 1894.

    DIED:

THEIR CHILDREN

DAUGHTER: HELEN LOUISE,

    BORN: ADVANCE, STODDARD COUNTY, MISSOURI.

    DATE: JANUARY 3, 1916.

    DIED:

BOWMAN GENEALOGY

Descendants of

JAMES REED BOWMAN   AND   LILLIE B. LIVELY
       1870   1873

FATHER: RICHARD EARL BOWMAN,
   BORN: BURFORDVILLE, MISSOURI.
   DATE: MAY 18, 1896.
   DIED:

MOTHER: MYRTLE CRAMER,
   BORN: JACKSON, MISSOURI.
   DATE: FEBRUARY 16, 1896,
   DIED:

THEIR CHILDREN

SON: JAMES WILSON,
   BORN: JACKSON, MISSOURI.
   DATE: NOVEMBER 19, 1914.
   DIED:

DAUGHTER: MARGARET,
   BORN: JACKSON, MISSOURI
   DATE: JANUARY 26, 1916.
   DIED:

DAUGHTER: VIRGINIA LEE,
   BORN: JACKSON, MISSOURI
   DATE: AUGUST 2, 1925.
   DIED:

BOWMAN GENEALOGY

Descendants of

RICHARD EARL BOWMAN AND MYRTLE CRAMER
1896   1896

FATHER: JAMES WILSON BOWMAN

    BORN: JACKSON, MISSOURI

    DATE: NOVEMBER 19, 1914.

    DIED:

MOTHER: EDNA RUTH DAVIS,

    BORN: BRAGGADOCIO, MISSOURI.

    DATE: JULY 21, 1906

    DIED:

THEIR CHILDREN

SON: JAMES WILSON, 2nd

    BORN: JACKSON, MISSOURI
    (In Cape Girardeau, Mo Hospital.)

    DATE: OCTOBER 15, 1939

    DIED:

DAUGHTER: EDNA ANN,

    BORN: JACKSON, MISSOURI
    (In Cape Girardeau, Mo Hospital.)

    DATE: September 6, 1943

    DIED:

BOWMAN   GENEALOGY
Descendants   of
RICHARD EARL BOWMAN   AND   MYRTLE CRAMER
         1896   1896

FATHER: HUBERT HARLICE COATES.
    BORN: EAST PRAIRIE, MISSOURI.
    DATE: SEPTEMBER 29, 1909
    DIED:

MOTHER: MARGARET, BOWMAN.
    BORN: JACKSON, MISSOURI
    DATE: JANUARY 26, 1916
    DIED:
===============================
            THEIR   CHILDREN

DAUGHTER: MARGARET ANN,
    BORN: DEERING, MISSOURI.
    DATE: SEPTEMBER 26, 1939
    DIED:

DAUGHTER: EMMA JO,
    BORN: SIKESTON, MISSOURI,
            (In Cape Girardeau, Mo Hospital.)
    DATE: AUGUST 23, 1945.
    DIED:

168

BOWMAN GENEALOGY

Descendants of

RICHARD EARL BOWMAN AND MYRTLE CRAMER
1896   1896

FATHER: JAMES HENRY B. TIMBERLAKE

     BORN: IN ENGLAND

     DATE   JUNE 11, 1924

     DIED:

MOTHER: VIRGINIA LEE BOWMAN,

     BORN: JACKSON, MISSOURI.

     DATE: AUGUST 2, 1925.

     DIED:

THEIR CHILDREN

DAUGHTER: SHARON LEE,

     BORN: JACKSON, MISSOURI
                 (In Cape Girardeau, Mo Hospital.)

     DATE: DECEMBER 11, 1945

     DIED:

SON: JAMES RICHARD,

     BORN: JACKSON, MISSOURI.
                 (In Cape Girardeau, Mo Hospital)

     DATE: MARCH 19, 1948.

     DIED:

BOWMAN GENEALOGY

Descendants of

JAMES REED BOWMAN   AND   LILLIE B. LIVELY
       1870   1873

FATHER: RAY S. DUNCAN,
    BORN: DIXON, KENTUCKY
    DATE: OCTOBER 16, 1905
    DIED:

MOTHER: ANICE LILYAN BOWMAN,
    BORN: BURFORDVILLE, MISSOURI.
    DATE: OCTOBER 6, 1900
    DIED:

THEIR CHILDREN

SON: RAY BOWMAN,
    BORN: CAPE GIRARDEAU, MISSOURI.
    DATE: NOVEMBER 19, 1935.
    DIED:

BOWMAN   GENEALOGY

Descendants of

JAMES REED BOWMAN   AND   LILLIE B. LIVELY
       1870   1873

FATHER: ROBERT BRYCE GOODWIN,
   BORN: LUTESVILLE, MISSOURI.
   DATE: JANUARY 10, 1902
   DIED:

MOTHER: MYRTLE MARGUERITE BOWMAN
   BORN: ADVANCE, MISSOURI
   DATE: OCTOBER 31, 1903
   DIED:

+ + + + + + + + + +++ + + + ++ + + ++ + + + + + ++ +

           THEIR CHILDREN

SON: ROBERT BRYCE, 2nd
   BORN: JACKSON, MISSOURI
   DATE: MAY 9, 1925
   DIED:

SON: JAMES LEE,
   BORN: JACKSON, MISSOURI
   DATE: JANUARY 17, 1928
   DIED:

SON: LANE ALDEN,
   BORN: JACKSON, MISSOURI
   DATE: OCTOBER 9, 1929
   DIED:

BOWMAN GENEALOGY
Descendants of
ROBERT BRYCE GOODWIN AND MYRTLE MARGUERITE BOWMAN
1902   1903

FATHER: ROBERT BRYCE GOODWIN, 2nd
- BORN: JACKSON, MISSOURI
- DATE: MAY 9, 1925
- DIED:

MOTHER: CAROL ANN DUNN,
- BORN: BERCH TREE, MISSOURI
- DATE: JULY 15, 1928
- DIED:

Married August 8, 1950.

++

THEIR CHILDREN:

DAUGHTER: TERESA ANN,
- BORN: CAPE GIRARDEAU, MISSOURI.
- DATE: AUGUST 25, 1955.
- DIED:

BOWMAN GENEALOGY

Descendants of
ROBERT BRYCE GOODWIN AND MYRTLE MARGUERITE BOWMAN
1902   1903

FATHER: JAMES LEE GOODWIN,   S/Sgt in U.S.Air Force.
- BORN: JACKSON, MISSOURI.
- DATE: JANUARY 17, 1928
- DIED:

Married June 19, 1950

MOTHER: MARY ERNEST CLACK
- BORN: EAST PRAIRIE, MISSOURI
- DATE: SEPTEMBER 19, 1927
- DIED:

++

THEIR CHILDREN:

SON: JAMES LEE, 2nd
- BORN: SAN ANTONIO, TEXAS
- DATE: SEPTEMBER 29, 1951
- DIED:

DAUGHTER: CATHRYN LANE,
- BORN: SAN ANTONIO, TEXAS
- DATE: JULY 10, 1953
- DIED:

BOWMAN   GENEALOGY   173.

Descendants of

ROBERT BRYCE GOODWIN   AND   MYRTLE MARGUERITE BOWMAN
          1902   1903

FATHER: LANE ALDEN GOODWIN   Lieut- U.S.Airborne
    BORN: JACKSON, MISSOURI:
    DATE: OCTOBER 9, 1929
    DIED:
    Married August 10, 1953.

MOTHER: LINDA BEEBE,
    BORN: SPARTA, WISCONSIN.
    DATE: NOVEMBER 16, 1934
    DIED:

++

THEIR CHILDREN

SON: THOMAS LANE,
    BORN: SPARTA, WISCONSIN
    DATE: JULY 30, 1954.
    DIED:

DAUGHTER: KIMBERLY ANN,
    BORN: COLUMBIA, MISSOURI.
    DATE: FEBRUARY 2, 1956.
    DIED:

BOWMAN GENEALOGY
Descendants of
BENJAMIN LEE BOWMAN AND ELIZA JANE FORD
1837   1840

FATHER: THOMAS FORD BOWMAN,
- BORN: IN CAPE GIRARDEAU COUNTY, MISSOURI
- DATE: NOVEMBER 6, 1872.
- DIED: DECEMBER 27, 1935.

MOTHER: MINNIE MARIE VAN DOREN,
- BORN: LEOPOLD, MISSOURI
- DATE: SEPTEMBER 27, 1872
- DIED: APRIL 2, 1953

++

+ THEIR CHILDREN +

SON: CHARLIE WELLS,
- BORN: LEOPOLD, MISSOURI
- DATE: JUNE 3, 1901.
- DIED:

SON: MILTON PAUL,
- BORN: LITTLE ROCK, ARKANSAS
- DATE: FEBRUARY 26, 1903
- DIED:

BOWMAN GENEALOGY

Descendants of

THOMAS FORD BOWMAN AND **MINNIE MARIE VAN DOREN**
1872   1872

(FIRST MARRIAGE)

FATHER: CHARLIE WELLS BOWMAN

      BORN: LEOPOLD, MISSOURI   (Divorced)

      DATE: JUNE 3, 1901.

      DIED:
              (Married at Cairo, Illinois April 28, 1923.)

MOTHER: FERN MARIE SCOTT,

      BORN: MOREHOUSE, MISSOURI   (Divorced)

      DATE: SEPTEMBER 30, 1900

      DIED:

(NO CHILDREN BY THE ABOVE MARRIAGE)

The writer is unable to locate the where-a-bouts of CHARLIE WELLS BOWMAN.

The last heard of him was in St Louis, Missouri where his brother Milton Paul now lives.

It was learned that his second marriage was to Gale Townsend.

His third marriage was to a woman whose first name was NITA ?? and to whom they had two boys by the name of Tommy, and Sammy.

His fourth marriage was to Leona Cavanaugh.

All dates in connection with these persons, and marriages are unknown at the present writing.

We are sorry we are unable to complete his records due to our inability to contact him.

                                          The Historian.

BOWMAN GENEALOGY

Descendants of

THOMAS FORD BOWMAN AND MINNIE MARIE VAN DOREN
1872   1872

FATHER: MILTON PAUL BOWMAN
  BORN: LITTLE ROCK, ARKANSAS
  DATE FEBRUARY 26, 1903
  DIED:

MOTHER: VELMA MARY CHILTON
  BORN: DES ARC, MISSOURI (IRON COUNTY)
  DATE: JULY 5, 1911
  DIED:

+ + + + + + + + + + + + + +++ + + + ++ ++ +

NO CHILDREN.

BOWMAN GENEALOGY
Descendants of

BENJAMIN LEE BOWMAN AND ELIZA JANE FORD
1837 1840

FATHER: JOSEPH MAPLE BOWMAN
    BORN: MARBLE HILL, BOLLINGER COUNTY, MISSOURI,
    DATE: JUNE 12, 1877
    DIED: JANUARY 31, 1952
  (Married on September 15, 1901.)

MOTHER: LILLIE DONALDSON,
    BORN: RIDGEWAY, ILLINOIS
    DATE: APRIL 6, 1883.
    DIED: DECEMBER 1904

++
+ NO CHILDREN +

BOWMAN GENEALOGY

Descendants of
BENJAMIN LEE BOWMAN AND ELIZA JANE FORD
1837   1840

FATHER: JOSEPH MAPLE BOWMAN

    BORN: MARBLE HILL, BOLLINGER COUNTY, MISSOURI.

    DATE: JUNE 12, 1877

    DIED: JANUARY 31, 1952
    (Married July 19, 1905.)
At Bastrop, Louisiana, by the Rev. S.D. Almon, Pastor of the
First Baptist Church. Wittnesses; Tom Turner, and Mrs. S.D. Almon.

MOTHER: MINNIE I. BRODNAX.

    BORN: BASTROP, LOUISIANA

    DATE: JUNE 15, 1882

    DIED: NOV 13 1955

++
+ **THEIR CHILDREN** +

DAUGHTER: LILLIE B,

    BORN: VIDALIA, LOUISIANA

    DATE: MARCH 20, 1906

    DIED:

SON: BENJAMIN LEE,

    BORN: ROSWELL, NEW MEXICO

    DATE: JUNE 30, 1907

    DIED:

SON: EM HARLAN,

    BORN: ROSWELL, NEW MEXICO

    DATE: DECEMBER 8, 1909.

    DIED:

DAUGHTER: ADELAIDE,
    BORN: BROWNWOOD, TEXAS
    DATE: JUNE 20, 1919
    DIED:

BOWMAN		GENEALOGY

Descendants of

JOSEPH MAPLE BOWMAN	AND	MINNIE I. BRODNAX
      1877						1882

FATHER:		LEWIS C. YATES,

    BORN:	McCAULEY, TEXAS

    DATE:	MAY 30, 1906

    DIED:

MOTHER:		LILLIE B BOWMAN,

    BORN:	VIDALIA, LOUISIANA

    DATE:	MARCH 20, 1906.

    DIED:

++

– NO CHILDREN –

A BOWMAN GENEALOGY

Decendants of
JOSEPH MAPLE BOWMAN   AND   MINNIE I. BRODNAX
1877   1882

FATHER: BENJAMIN LEE BOWMAN
- BORN: ROSWELL, NEW MEXICO
- DATE: JUNE 30, 1907
- DIED:

MOTHER: BERNICE IRENE HAILE
- BORN: KINGSLAND, TEXAS
- DATE: MARCH 22, 1911
- DIED:

++

THEIR CHILDREN

DAUGHTER: BARBARA LOUISE,
- BORN: BROWNWOOD, TEXAS
- DATE: OCTOBER 7, 1927
- DIED:

SON: BENJAMIN LEE, Jr
- BORN: BROWNWOOD, TEXAS
- DATE: JULY 30, 1929
- DIED:

BOWMAN   GENEALOGY

Decendants of

BENJAMIN LEE BOWMAN, Sr AND BERNICE IRENE HAILE
1907   1911

FATHER: JAY M. AXTELL,
  BORN: FORT WORTH, TEXAS
  DATE: JANUARY 9, 1922
  DIED:

MOTHER: BARBARA LOUISE BOWMAN,
  BORN: BROWNWOOD, TEXAS
  DATE: OCTOBER 7, 1927
  DIED:

++
+ THEIR CHILDREN +

SON: RONNIE,
  BORN: SAN ANGELO, TEXAS
  DATE: JANUARY 6, 1944
  DIED:

SON: TONY LEE,
  BORN: SAN ANGELO, TEXAS
  DATE: DECEMBER 27, 1947
  DIED:

181-A

BOWMAN GENEALOGY

Descendants of

BENJAMIN LEE BOWMAN, Sr   AND   BERNICE IRENE HAILE
        1907   1911

FATHER: BENJAMIN LEE BOWMAN, JR
    BORN: BROWNWOOD, TEXAS
    DATE: JULY 30, 1929.
    DIED:
    Married: June 5, 1955.

MOTHER: SHARON KAYE HARWOOD.
    BORN: WINTERS, TEXAS.
    DATE: JUNE 23, 1937.
    DIED:

        THEIR CHILDREN

SON: BARRY LEE,
    BORN: SAN ANGELO, TEXAS
    DATE: APRIL 3, 1956.
    DIED:

    BORN:
    DATE:
    DIED:

    BORN:
    DATE:
    DIED:

BOWMAN GENEALOGY

Descendants of

JOSEPH MAPLE BOWMAN AND MINNIE I. BRODNAX
1877   1882

FATHER: EM HARLAN BOWMAN
    BORN: ROSWELL, NEW MEXICO   (FIRST MARRIAGE)
    DATE: DECEMBER 8, 1909   (Divorced)
    DIED:

MOTHER: MARY LOUISE JONES
    BORN: WAXAHACHIE, TEXAS.
    DATE: 1908.
    DIED:

+ +
+ THEIR CHILDREN +

DAUGHTER: JOE ANN,
    BORN: BROWNWOOD, TEXAS.
    DATE: MARCH 3, 1931.
    DIED:

BOWMAN GENEALOGY

Descendants of

EM HARLAND BOWMAN AND MARY LOUISE JONES

FATHER: ROBERT E. MILLER.
    BORN: BEAUMONT, TEXAS
    DATE: MARCH 1, 1928.
    DIED:

MOTHER: JOE ANN BOWMAN.
    BORN: BROWNWOOD, TEXAS.
    DATE: MARCH 3, 1931.
    DIED:

++

+ THEIR CHILDREN +

SON: ROBERT E. MILLER, JR
    BORN: SAN ANTONIO, TEXAS
    DATE: APRIL 8, 1954.
    DIED:

SON: RICHARD ALAN,
    BORN: FELIXSTOWE, SUFFOLK, ENGLAND.
    DATE: SEPTEMBER 23, 1955.
    DIED:

BOWMAN   GENEALOGY

Descendants of

JOSEPH MAPLE BOWMAN   AND   MINNIE I. BRODNAX
1877   1882

FATHER: EM HARLAN BOWMAN
    BORN: ROSWELL, NEW MEXICO
    DATE: DECEMBER 8, 1909
    DIED:

(SECOND MARRIAGE)

MOTHER: NEVA CATHERINE COX,
    BORN: (ENERGY, TEXAS
    DATE: MAY 14 1921.
    DIED:

++

+ THEIR CHILDREN +

SON: JOE THOMAS,
    BORN: SAN FRANCISCO, CALIFORNIA
    DATE: JUNE 21, 1944
    DIED:

BOWMAN GENEALOGY
Descendants of
JOSEPH MAPLE BOWMAN   AND   MINNIE I. BRODNAX
    1877   1882

FATHER: JAMES LEO HARVEY
    BORN: BELOIT, KANSAS
    DATE: DECEMBER 22, 1919
    DIED:
             (Divorced)

MOTHER: ADELAIDE BOWMAN
    BORN: BROWNWOOD, TEXAS
    DATE: JUNE 20, 1919
    DIED:
             (First Marriage)

++

+THEIR CHILDREN+

DAUGHTER: JAN IRIS,
    BORN: BROWNWOOD, TEXAS
    DATE: JULY   27, 1940
    DIED:

SON: JAMES MICHAEL,
    BORN: BRADY, TEXAS
    DATE: JANUARY 23, 1945
    DIED:

BOWMAN GENEALOGY

Descendants of

JOSEPH MAPLE BOWMAN AND MINNIE I. BRODNAX
1877   1882

FATHER: R.P. LYNN,

     BORN:

     DATE:

     DIED: (Divorced)

MOTHER: ADELAIDE BOWMAN HARVEY

     BORN: BROWNWOOD, TEXAS

     DATE: JUNE 20, 1919

     DIED:
       (Second Marriage.)

++

+ THEIR CHILDREN +

DAUGHTER: LINDA SUE,

     BORN: BRADY, TEXAS

     DATE: AUGUST 26, 1947

     DIED:

THE NAME OF ADELAIDE LYNN AND LINDA SUE LYNN CHANGED BY COURT ORDER TO: ADELAIDE HARVEY AND LINDA SUE HARVEY:

THE THREE CHILDREN OF ADELAIDE HARVEY BEING:
   Jan Iris Harvey
   James Michael Harvey, and
   Linda Sue Harvey

ADELAIDE HARVEY is now a widow, living in Brady, Texas. Her three children reside with her in Brady, Texas.

BOWMAN GENEALOGY 186

Descendants of

BENJAMIN LEE BOWMAN AND ELIZA JANE FORD
1837   1840

FATHER: WILBUR TALLEY BOWMAN

    BORN: MARBLE HILL, BOLLINGER COUNTY, MISSOURI

    DATE: DECEMBER 22, 1878

    DIED: JUNE 29, 1940

(Married September 15, 1901.)

MOTHER: HATTIE DONALDSON,

    BORN: RIDGEWAY, ILLINOIS

    DATE: JUNE 6, 1881

    DIED:

(Married September 15, 1901 near Dexter, Mo.)

+ THEIR CHILDREN +

SON: JAMES D.

    BORN: MER ROUGE, LOUISIANA

    DATE: JANUARY 7, 1903

    DIED:

DAUGHTER: LILLIE B.

    BORN: CLARKS, LOUISIANA

    DATE: JUNE 14, 1904

    DIED:

SON: WILBUR J.

    BORN: SIKESTON, MISSOURI

    DATE: JUNE 16, 1906

    DIED:

SON: WOODROW W.

    BORN: DEXTER, MISSOURI

    DATE: MARCH 12, 1914.

    DIED:

BOWMAN GENEALOGY
Descendants of
WILBUR TALLEY BOWMAN AND HATTIE DONALDSON
1878   1881

FATHER: JAMES DONALDSON BOWMAN
- BORN: MER ROUGE, LOUISIANA
- DATE: JANUARY 7, 1903
- DIED:

Married January 30, 1926
Major in U.S. Air Corp RETIRED.

MOTHER: CATHERINE ANNA DODGE,
- BORN: MILWAUKEE, WISCONSIN.
- DATE: AUGUST 16, 1903
- DIED:

++

+ THEIR CHILDREN +

DAUGHTER: CATHERINE ANNA,
- BORN: SAN FRANCISCO, CALIFORNIA
- DATE: APRIL 27, 1930
- DIED:

DAUGHTER: PATRICIA ANN,
- BORN: SACRAMENTO, CALIFORNIA
- DATE: JANUARY 13, 1943
- DIED:

BOWMAN GENEALOGY
Descendants of
JAMES DONALDSON BOWMAN AND CATHERINE ANNA DODGE
1903   1903

FATHER: GLENN PATRICK SEYFERTH,
- BORN: CHIPPEWA FALLS, WISCONSIN
- DATE: OCTOBER 1929
- DIED:

(Married May 10, 1946)

MOTHER: CATHERINE ANNA BOWMAN,
- BORN: SAN FRANCISCO, CALIFORNIA
- DATE: APRIL 27, 1930
- DIED:

++
+ THEIR CHILDREN +

DAUGHTER: CATHERINE DIANA,
- BORN: PALO ALTO, CALIFORNIA
- DATE: MARCH 9, 1947
- DIED:

DAUGHTER: SUSAN ELIZABETH,
- BORN: SAN FRANCISCO, CALIFORNIA
- DATE: APRIL 2, 1950
- DIED:

SON: GLEN PATRICK, Jr
- BORN: FORT DIX, NEW JERSEY
- DATE: MAY 10, 1953
- DIED:

BOWMAN GENEALOGY

Descendants of

WILBUR TALLEY BOWMAN AND HATTIE DONALDSON
　　　1878　　　　　　　　　　　1881

FATHER:　　　THOMAS LAWRENCE HALLAHAN.

　　BORN:　CLOVIS, CALIFORNIA

　　DATE:　JULY 16, 1905.

　　DIED:

MOTHER:　　LILLIE B. BOWMAN,

　　BORN:　CLARKS, LOUISIANA

　　DATE:　JUNE 14, 1904

　　DIED:
　　　　　　(Married April 16, 1927)
++

+ THEIR CHILDREN +

DAUGHTER:　　CAROLE JEAN,

　　BORN:　MERCED, CALIFORNIA

　　DATE:　JANUARY 12, 1931

　　DIED:

BOWMAN GENEALOGY
Descendants of
WILBUR TALLEY BOWMAN AND HATTIE DONALDSON
1878   1881

FATHER: WILBUR JOHN BOWMAN
   BORN: SIKESTON, MISSOURI
   DATE: JUNE 18, 1906
   DIED:

MOTHER: MARY CATHERINE GUBBINS.
   BORN: CHICAGO, ILLINOIS
   DATE: AUGUST 28, 1906.
   DIED:
            (Married October 12, 1936.)

++
                + THEIR CHILDREN +

DAUGHTER: MARY CATHERINE,
   BORN: SAN FRANCISCO, CALIFORNIA
   DATE: NOV 11, 1937
   DIED:

SON: W. JOHN JOSEPH,
   BORN   PHOENIX, ARIZONA
   DATE: NOVEMBER 5, 1939
   DIED:

SON: L. JAMES JOSEPH,
   BORN: PHOENIX, ARIZONA
   DATE: OCTOBER 14, 1940
   DIED:

DAUGHTER: MARGARET MARY,
   BORN: PHOENIX, ARIZONA
   DATE: JUNE 29, 1942
   DIED:

SON: ROBERT JOSEPH,
   BORN: SAN FRANCISCO, CALIFORNIA
   DATE: MAY 25, 1946
   DIED:

BOWMAN   GENEALOGY

Descendants   of

WILBUR TALLEY BOWMAN   AND   HATTIE DONALDSON
    1878   1881

FATHER: WOODROW W. BOWMAN
    BORN: DEXTER, MISSOURI
    DATE: MARCH 12, 1914
    DIED:
          (Married June 1, 1935.)

MOTHER: BILLIE HARRISON
    BORN: SAN FRANCISCO, CALIFORNIA
    DATE: OCTOBER 11, 1915.
    DIED:

++
+ THEIR CHILDREN +

DAUGHTER: JOAN ELIZABETH,
    BORN: SAN FRANCISCO, CALIFORNIA
    DATE: JUNE 25, 1938.
    DIED:

BOWMAN GENEALOGY

Descendants of

BENJAMIN LEE BOWMAN AND ELIZA JANE FORD
         1837   1840

FATHER: THOMAS ALEXANDER ABERNATHY
- BORN: POCAHONTAS, MISSOURI
- DATE: NOVEMBER 11, 1870
- DIED: APRIL 6, 1938

MOTHER: ANNA BOWMAN
- BORN: MARBLE HILL, BOLLINGER COUNTY, MISSOURI.
- DATE: OCTOBER 20, 1880
- DIED: AUGUST 1, 1955.

+ THEIR CHILDREN +

DAUGHTER: LUELLA,
- BORN: MARBLE HILL, MISSOURI.
- DATE: MAY 4, 1901.
- DIED:

DAUGHTER: SARA LEE,
- BORN: SIKESTON, MISSOURI.
- DATE: FEBRUARY 7, 1905
- DIED: MAY 9, 1941.

DAUGHTER: GERALDINE,
- BORN: SIKESTON, MISSOURI.
- DATE: NOVEMBER 2, 1906.
- DIED:

BOWMAN GENEALOGY

Descendants of

Benjamin Lee Bowman and Eliza Jane Ford
1837   1840

THOMAS ALEXANDER ABERNATHY & ANNA BOWMAN

(Continued) from page 192.

DAUGHTER: ANNA,
    BORN: POCAHONTAS, MISSOURI.
    DATE: JANUARY 28, 1912.
    DIED:

DAUGHTER: MELVIN,
    BORN: SIKESTON, MISSOURI.
    DATE: JUNE 28, 1914.
    DIED:

SON: THOMAS ALEXANDER, JR
    BORN: SIKESTON, MISSOURI.
    DATE: AUGUST 10, 1916.
    DIED:

DAUGHTER: NETTIE JANE
    BORN: JOHNSON CITY, ILLINOIS.
    DATE: MARCH 24, 1921.
    DIED:

BOWMAN GENEALOGY

Descendants of

ANNA BOWMAN AND THOMAS ALEXANDER ABERNATHY
1880   1870

FATHER: JOHN D. McNABB, Sr
     BORN:
     DATE
     DIED:
(Divorced on JUNE 10, 1923 at St Louis, Mo.)

MOTHER: LUELLA ABERNATHY,
     BORN: MARBLE HILL, MISSOURI
     DATE: MAY 4, 1901.
     DIED:

+ THEIR CHILDREN +

SON: JOHN D, Jr
     BORN: JOHNSON CITY, ILLINOIS.
     DATE: NOVEMBER 15, 1920
     DIED:

BOWMAN GENEALOGY

Descendants of

ANNA BOWMAN AND **THOMAS ALEXANDER ABERNATHY**
1880   1870

FATHER: CHARLES HENRY BANES,
         BORN: MINE LA MOTTE, MISSOURI.
         DATE: DECEMBER 20, 1893.
         DIED: SEPTEMBER 19, 1952
            At St Louis, Missouri.

Married on June 11, 1924 at Johnson City, Ill.

MOTHER: LUELLA ABERNATHY (McNABB).
         BORN: MARBLE HILL, MISSOURI
         DATE: MAY 4, 1901.
         DIED:

(No children by this marriage.)

BOWMAN   GENEALOGY

Descendants   of

JOHN D.McNABB, Sr   AND   LUELLA ABERNATHY
1901

FATHER: JOHN D.McNABB, Jr

    BORN: JOHNSON CITY, ILLINOIS

    DATE: NOVEMBER 15, 1920

    DIED:

MOTHER: IRENE NUFER,

    BORN: ST LOUIS, MISSOURI

    DATE: JULY 23, 1928.

    DIED:

========================

THEIR CHILDREN

SON: KEVIN CHARLES,

    BORN: ST LOUIS, MISSOURI

    DATE: JULY 10, 1951.

    DIED:

DAUGHTER: MELLISSA LYNN,

    BORN: ST LOUIS, MISSOURI

    DATE: SEPTEMBER 5, 1953.

    DIED:

BOWMAN GENEALOGY
Descendants of
ANNA BOWMAN AND THOMAS ALEXANDER ABERNATHY
1880 1870

FATHER: JOSEPH NOSER.
- BORN: ROCKFORD, ILLINOIS
- DATE: OCTOBER 11, 1900.
- DIED: MARCH 8, 1937.

MOTHER: SARA LEE ABERNATHY.
- BORN: SIKESTON, MISSOURI
- DATE: FEBRUARY 7, 1905.
- DIED: MAY 9, 1941.

+ +
+ THEIR CHILDREN +

DAUGHTER: FRIEDA AGNES (Peggy),
- BORN: JOHNSON CITY, ILLINOIS.
- DATE: JULY 24, 1920.
- DIED:

BOWMAN GENEALOGY
Descendants of
JOSEPH NOSER and SARA LEE ABERNATHY
1900 1905

FATHER: AUDREY M. NELSON
    BORN: MILSTADT, ILLINOIS
    DATE: DECEMBER 31, 1918
    DIED:

(Married on August 17, 1937.)

MOTHER: FRIEDA AGNES (Peggy) NOSER.
    BORN: JOHNSON CITY, ILLINOIS.
    DATE: JULY 24, 1920.
    DIED:

+ +

+ THEIR CHILDREN +

SON: JOE LEE,
    BORN: ST LOUIS, MISSOURI
    DATE: JANUARY 8, 1943.
    DIED:

DAUGHTER: VICKE LYNN,
    BORN: CAIRO, ILLINOIS
    DATE: JANUARY 3, 1950.
    DIED:

BOWMAN   GENEALOGY

Descendants   of

ANNA BOWMAN   AND   THOMAS ALEXANDER ABERNATHY
  1880   1870

FATHER: FRED JACKSON.
    BORN: JACKSON, TENNESSEE.
    DATE: DECEMBER 24, 1895.
    DIED:

MOTHER: GERALDINE ABERNATHY.
    BORN: SIKESTON, MISSOURI.
    DATE: NOVEMBER 2, 1906
    DIED:

+ +

(NO CHILDREN)

BOWMAN   GENEALOGY
Descendants   of

ANNA BOWMAN   AND   THOMAS ALEXANDER ABERNATHY.
    1880   1870

FATHER: DAVID HUNTER.
    BORN   JOHNSON CITY, ILLINOIS.
    DATE: OCTOBER 12, 1910.
    DIED:

MOTHER: ANNA ABERNATHY.
    BORN: POCAHONTAS, MISSOURI.
    DATE: JANUARY 28, 1912.
    DIED:

+ ++
    + THEIR CHILDREN +

DAUGHTER: DIANE LEE,
    BORN: JOHNSON CITY, ILLINOIS
    DATE: SEPTEMBER 23, 1935.
    DIED:

DAUGHTER: JUDITH RAE,
    BORN: JOHNSON CITY, ILLINOIS.
    DATE: AUGUST 22, 1937.
    DIED:

BOWMAN   GENEALOGY

Descendants of

ANNA BOWMAN   AND   THOMAS ALEXANDER ABERNATHY.
   1880   1870

FATHER: SAMUEL MASSEY.
    BORN: TRUSSVILLE, ALABAMA
    DATE: JANUARY 28, 1916.
    DIED:

MOTHER: MELVIN ABERNATHY.
    BORN: SIKESTON, MISSOURI.
    DATE: JUNE 28, 1914.
    Died;

+ +
              + THEIR CHILDREN +

SON: THOMAS HERBERT,
    BORN: TRUSSVILLE, ALABAMA.
    DATE: JANUARY 31, 1939.
    DIED:

DAUGHTER: LINDA LOU.
    BORN: TRUSSVILLE, ALABAMA.
    DATE: APRIL 21, 1941.

BOWMAN GENEALOGY
Descendants of
ANNA BOWMAN AND THOMAS ALEXANDER ABERNATHY
1880   1870

FATHER: THOMAS A. ABERNATHY, Jr
- BORN: SIKESTON, MISSOURI.
- DATE: AUGUST 10, 1916.
- DIED:

MOTHER: EDYTHE WHITEHEAD.
- BORN: BIRMINGHAM, ALABAMA
- DATE: AUGUST 8, 1918.
- DIED:

+ +
+ THEIR CHILDREN +

DAUGHTER: CHARLSIE LOU
- BORN: BREMEN, GEORGIA
- DATE: APRIL 21, 1942.
- DIED:

DAUGHTER: PEGGY ANN,
- BORN: BOWDON, GEORGIA.
  (Jubal Watts Memorial Hospital)
- DATE: MAY 19, 1946.
- DIED:

BOWMAN GENEALOGY

Descendants of
ANNA BOWMAN AND THOMAS ALEXANDER ABERNATHY
1880   1870

FATHER: JOHN H. HACKNEY,
- BORN: BARDWELL, KENTUCKY.
- DATE: MARCH 10, 1922.
- DIED:

MOTHER: NETTIE JANE ABERNATHY.
- BORN: MARCH 24, 1921.
- DATE: JOHNSON CITY, ILLINOIS.
- DIED:

+ ++++ + + +

+ THEIR CHILDREN +

SON: JOHN H. HACKNEY, Jr
- BORN: ST LOUIS, MISSOURI.
- DATE: DECEMBER 12, 1947.
- DIED:

SON: THOMAS KELLEY,
- BORN: ST LOUIS, MISSOURI.
- DATE: MAY 2, 1949.
- DIED:

DAUGHTER: SALLY ANN,
- BORN: ST LOUIS, MISSOURI.
- DATE: JUNE 12, 1951.
- DIED:

Printed in the USA
CPSIA information can be obtained
at www.ICGtesting.com
LVHW081216061023
760240LV00022B/192